GIVING UP
WITHOUT
GIVING UP

GIVING UP WITHOUT GIVING UP

Meditation and Depressions

JIM GREEN

BLOOMSBURY CONTINUUM
LONDON · NEW YORK · OXFORD · NEW DELHI · SYDNEY

BLOOMSBURY CONTINUUM
Bloomsbury Publishing Plc
50 Bedford Square, London, WC1B 3DP, UK

First published in Great Britain 2019

A catalogue record for this book is available from the British Library

Library of Congress Cataloguing-in-Publication data has been applied for

ISBN: TPB: 978-1-4729-5745-0; EPDF: 978-1-4729-5744-3; EPUB: 978-1-4729-5746-7

2 4 6 8 10 9 7 5 3 1

Typeset by Newgen KnowledgeWorks Pvt. Ltd., Chennai, India
Printed and bound in Great Britain by CPI Group (UK) Ltd, Croydon CR0 4YY

To find out more about our authors and books visit www.bloomsbury.com
and sign up for our newsletters

For Kath

CONTENTS

'Set your troubled hearts at rest'

IN THE DARK

There is an old tale that crops up, with slight variations, at different times and across many cultures. The version I remember is an American cartoon strip from the 1940s. In it, a dishevelled man, who has clearly taken on board a good number of drinks in the course of the evening, is searching earnestly for something under the light of a solitary lamp-post. A policeman approaches and asks what he's looking for. 'My keys,' slurs the searcher. 'Well, where did you lose them?' asks the policeman. 'Back there,' comes the answer, with a jerked thumb over the shoulder indicating the darkness further up the street. 'Then what are you doing looking here?' asks the puzzled policeman. The drunk carries on scrutinizing the illuminated sidewalk. Slowly he gathers himself. 'Because the light is so much better here,' he patiently explains.

This little fable has always spoken eloquently to me about the touching determination with which we all tend to look in the wrong places. We are convinced that we can't find anything in the darkness, and anyway, it's a frightening place to be – we never know what or who might find *us* there. But deep down, very deep down, we know where it is – the key, the coin, the ring, the treasure that we lost. But we daren't go there. What to do? Often we get depressed. Yet there are ways that we can learn to be – and to see – in the dark. In my experience, meditation is just such a way.

When we're depressed we're nearly always being asked to loosen our grip on some long-cherished ideas and beliefs about who we are and how the world works. They might be so long-cherished that we are completely unaware they exist. Depression is the inarticulate desire for change. When it seems that we are powerless to change anything, the practice of meditation can begin to open us – perhaps for the first time – to authentic self-knowledge.

At times of depression we also tend to swing between an unbearable restlessness and a terrible feeling of being utterly stuck. Our thoughts turn in on themselves, repeatedly trying to unpick the same thickening network of mental knots. The internal monologue becomes so intense that we end up incommunicado, filled and surrounded by a wall of white noise.

Meditation offers a way of not being overwhelmed by these unhelpful states of consciousness. Rather than fighting it off at all costs, meditation can help us to be with our depression and to learn from it. The restlessness, complexity and noisiness that distort all of our lives can be met – and gently changed – by following this wisdom practice that will reawaken our innate experience of stillness, simplicity and silence. It is a way that guides us from the scorched desert that our aching heads and bodies have become, back to the heart that we thought we had lost forever. It opens us to living as fully as possible in both the darkness and the light.

WELCOME

Welcome to this book and to the shared experience of all those who have read it or are going to read it. If you've been drawn by the title, the chances are that you have experienced, or are experiencing, what at this point in human history, within an increasing number of cultures, we have agreed to call *depression*. Or perhaps you earn your living by being of service to people whose lives seem to be blocked and distorted by the experience (or apparent *non*-experience) that this word tries to describe. You may be concerned, even to the point of desperation, about a family member, a friend, a work colleague whose life seems paralysed, joyless and full of anguish. Or perhaps you simply feel an urgent call to engage, not just with a 'condition', but with *the* human condition – that mysterious invitation extended to all of us – of which depression is so surely and necessarily a part.

A word about the title. It contains some of the best advice I've ever heard. I was supervising a psychotherapist at the mental health and wellbeing project I was managing. He also happened to be a gardener and a Zen practitioner – a good portfolio. He said that this message – *give up without giving up* – was essentially what he offered to each of his clients in one way or another. Many years later, it still resonates for me. It seems to sum up, in an urgent and economical way, the essence of all the wisdom teachings. In the face of overwhelming personal anguish and defeat, it speaks to us even more directly. Stop struggling, let go of the story that has you trapped, accept that you are lost and that you don't know who you are. But keep going, only now in a direction of which you are (blessedly) no longer in total control.

Meditation can be a way of doing exactly that. It's a practical exploration of what it's like to release yourself – initially just for those 20 minutes or however long it lasts – from the desperate task of keeping the show on the road. The familiar strategies and stories, goals and preferences that have kept you going are clearly no longer working. What happens if, instead of ever more frantically trying to start it all up again, you simply *give up*? Meditation is a practice that can hold you and connect you, as you loosen your grip on everything that has brought you to this moment. This is giving up without giving up at its most immediate and personal.

The practice of meditation that I want to share with you has grown out of the sacred traditions of the world. It's a way of living the wisdom at the heart of them all, not just reading or thinking or talking about it. Too much disembodied thinking and talking may be part of what got us into this mess in the first place. The practice helps us to give up looking in the wrong place. Perhaps its true power lies in allowing us to stop looking altogether, as we start to simply *see*.

Depressions in the plural, rather than simple *depression*. I realized I didn't want to overlook the particular experience of countless individuals by just nodding through a word charged with all kinds of implications. *Depression* has been described as 'a vague term for a variety of states'. I'd go further and say that each depression is unique. There are as many *depressions* as there are people undergoing the experience of life-arresting despair. Even though I will often use the word *depression* throughout this book, the title is there as a reminder. Rather than focusing on an illness or a disease, I want us to pay attention to living persons: me and you.

So, all are welcome. And I'd encourage you to pause for a moment and welcome *yourself* to this particular adventure, this continuing of your exploration. For all the myriad things I don't know about you, what I *do* know is that you are reading these words and (probably) holding this book in your hands *in the present moment*. Everything takes place in this moment – the eternal, unrepeatable, astonishing and largely ignored Now. So, encouraging you to welcome yourself is one more way of inviting you to become *present*, just as you are, exactly where you are. There is nothing grand or special about this. It's simply a matter of opening our attention, noticing, acknowledging and accepting. The muffled jolt of a van in the street, the faint hum of the heater, a nagging pain in the lower back, a pool of light from the Anglepoise lamp falling onto the keyboard. Every second that we are alive is an opportunity to expose ourselves to the radiance of the present moment. But this isn't easy – in fact, it can feel utterly impossible – when every second seems to last an eternity and is full of an unnameable but agonizing pain. Which is another attempt to describe the indescribable experience of depression.

One further – and crucial – welcome needs to be extended: to this very experience itself, the one that currently goes under the name of *depression*. Anyone who has been through it will readily tell you that, at its most intense, it is the worst thing that a human being can experience. A living death devoid of meaning and all vitality, filled with crushing physical symptoms, dread of everything and – usually – profound self-condemnation. How – and why – would we welcome that? Well, that's what this book hopes to help you explore. For now, perhaps it's enough to answer the question by saying that we need to welcome depression simply because – like Mount Everest – it's there. If we deny it, fight with it or rush to bundle it out of the door, we can be sure that no good will come of it. What's more, it won't have a chance to do its transformative work.

This doesn't mean that we should be actively seeking out depression and the events that cause us to feel that way. No one needs to be sending out those particular invitations. Nor will most of us feel remotely able to celebrate the onset of the inner bleakness and chaos that characterize depression. At the time that it is happening, pain is simply pain and suffering is suffering. It feels pointless and endless. But perhaps, just perhaps, we might be able to shift our relationship to it. Change our experience of the experience. What if we were to have the same attitude to our own experiences that St Benedict encourages the monks to have in his Rule, when he says that all guests who present themselves are to be welcomed as Christ? What if we experiment with understanding that our depression itself is Christ? What happens then?

What is unlooked for, what is uninvited and what is – instinctively – unwelcome and rejected in our lives can be the very agent of transformation that enables our growth to continue. (It's worth remembering that a central experience of Jesus' life on earth was that of rejection.) Richard Rohr, one of the great contemplative teachers of our day, says that there are only two paths of authentic human transformation: prayer (meditation) and suffering. Sometimes we will forget to pray but – he reassures us – don't worry, there will always be suffering.

Some of our suffering is a given, but our response to it is not. In Benedict's encouragement to his monks there is more than just simple hospitality (though this – how we treat each other – is recognized by all the wisdom traditions as the supreme human value). Fully understood, Benedict's words echo what lies at the heart of the Buddha's central teaching: the Four Ennobling Truths. One of them tells us that we suffer because we are driven by craving and by fear. We like *her*, we don't like *him*; I prefer *this* to *that*. And soon (from the moment of our birth, in fact) these preferences solidify, *become* us, and then turn into a quietly desperate matter of life and death. Both the Buddha and Jesus invite us to do it differently. They ask us whether we are able to be present to what everything in us is screaming out to reject. Even better, they show us a way that this can be done. If we can sit and let the seemingly impossible happen – to welcome what is at first so deeply unwelcome – then we might give ourselves a chance to learn something and to see something completely unexpected.

This reception and befriending of whatever seems to threaten our very existence is at the heart of any real human growth and healing. Most of us spend most of our time determined to do just the opposite. This was the thinking of the Buddha's parents, who tried to shield him as a young man from all knowledge of disease, ageing and death. The Awakened One's parents are still powerfully at work in the image-systems of contemporary culture and within our own thought-patterns and evasions. But it was only through a deep, experiential and embodied *knowing* of disease, ageing and death that the Buddha emptied them of their power over him.

This chosen intimacy with what is unwelcome is the golden key that we each hold in our hands. It is through such a voluntary relationship with our rejected shadow (another name for *the unwelcome*) that we can start to ask questions of death, ageing and disease, rather than being the mere victims of their apparently relentless interrogation. Illness might then even come to be experienced as a way to a greater healing. Describing depression as an illness or disease is one of my own least favourite ways of talking about this set of experiences, though I know such an understanding has been authentically helpful for others. But if we *do* choose to consider these sometimes terrifying episodes of desolation and isolation in our lives as an illness, then perhaps we might think of it as the kind of affliction that Nietzsche described: an illness full of a future.

For many, myself included, a much more encouraging and empowering understanding of depression is that, rather than it being simply an *illness*, we can most accurately think of it as *something that we do*. Which is not to say that it is our fault, or just another silly weakness, something to punish ourselves for and so – here comes a familiar vicious circle – to get even more depressed about. It is something that – as vulnerable human beings – we can hardly help ourselves from doing. There is always – always – a reason for our depression. In our anguish, we can get trapped in blaming others or blaming the world. All too often this turns into blaming ourselves. But at the heart of healing is the discovery of forgiveness. You might need to get very, very angry first or be helped to feel the full extent of your sadness, but – beyond that – the gift of forgiveness waits for you. You are not at fault – you are just temporarily stuck in the middle of a half-completed strategy. Because, if depression is something that we do, then it is also something that we can *undo*, though that undoing might take a form that we can't possibly imagine from the vantage point of this particular Now. And it might mean sitting with it, being with it, with all the courage that you can find in yourself, and that others offer to you, so that the depression can carry out its precious work.

Why and how we do depression is something that this book explores. How we *undo* it, as patiently and wisely as possible, is at the heart of the book. There are many ways to work and to play with depression (yes, even with depression, that strange experience which *seems* utterly devoid of the constructive or the playful). We can – if we are supported – work and play our way through it by offering ourselves as much of a recovery package as possible, because that is what we need and that is what works: talking and listening to others – friends or mental health professionals; taking care of your body – its need for exercise, fresh air and healthy food; continuing with whatever meaningful activity you are capable of; and sometimes giving yourself permission to stop, to apparently do nothing, to recover. Whatever connects or reconnects you with something else and with others – though it may seem at the time so slight, so tentative and so insignificant – is the golden thread that enables you to give up without giving up.

Meditation can be part of your healing *undoing*. I don't offer it, by itself, as a *cure* for depression. There are times when it will be essential to seek the help of medical professionals and all the support that they can offer. There is also much work for us to do as we journey into self-knowledge, alongside a therapist or counsellor – if we are lucky enough to have access to such a person. Or simply through the work of living as reflectively and patiently as we can. The practice of meditation can underpin and embrace all of this healing work. And one of our discoveries along the way might be the difference between *healing* and *a cure*.

In this book I hope to encourage you as you explore this simple but transformative practice, and to support you as you find out where it sits for you in relation to the experiences we call depression. I hope we can together ask what depression's other names might be, and extend our curiosity to what happens when our practice – as it will – invites us to let go of all the names we think we have ever known. And the vital part of this is that we are doing it *together*. As has thrillingly been said of this practice: 'meditation creates community'. That is one of the reasons why it might just be exactly the right treatment for depression.

At various points throughout the book there are invitations to stop reading and to meditate. Of course, that is a matter of choice for you. When and where (and if) you decide to do it is up to you. The invitations are there as a reminder to all of us that reading and writing about meditation is not meditation. Experience is the real teacher.

Welcome.

THE GUEST HOUSE

This being human is a guest house.
Every morning a new arrival.

A joy, a depression, a meanness,
some momentary awareness comes
as an unexpected visitor.

Welcome and entertain them all!
Even if they're a crowd of sorrows,
who violently sweep your house
empty of its furniture,
still, treat each guest honorably.
He may be clearing you out
for some new delight.

The dark thought, the shame, the malice,
meet them at the door laughing,
and invite them in.

Be grateful for whoever comes,
because each has been sent
as a guide from beyond.

Rumi

LEARNING TO BEGIN

I was very excited. On my two previous trips to California I had been to San Francisco and other parts of the West Coast, but I had never made it to L.A. – mythical home of angels, starlets and the dreams of all the world. Now I found myself at a hilltop Catholic convent with views over the seemingly limitless, sun-parched sprawl of Los Angeles. The city of stars shimmered below me in its wispy shroud of smog. I was here for a Zen–Christian retreat.

That was the initial reason for my excitement. Since being given my first book about this manifestation of Buddhism (birthday present, 1977) I had instinctively known that the meeting between Zen and the Christian contemplative tradition was the place where I was going to find – and then repeatedly lose, and then find again – my path. The immediacy of Zen, its startling directness, its readiness to dissolve all forms and formulations appealed to me, but so did what little I then knew about the Christian way of contemplation. Zen was attractive, because it was exotic and *other* – much more so then, only 26 years distant from today. It was counter-cultural, it broke all the rules, it was what your mother and father had no chance of understanding. But there was also the pull of my own tradition, the lightly worn, almost accidental Anglicanism of my parents, to say nothing of the entire Christian heritage of the West. I didn't want to leave my cultural and emotional home that irrevocably. As D. W. Winnicott, the celebrated child psychotherapist, said of children (and all of us), 'It is a joy to be hidden and a disaster not to be found.' I may well at that time have been seeking to hide in Zen, but I secretly knew that I wanted to find, and be found by, 'my' Christian tradition. And after all, hadn't His Holiness the Fourteenth Dalai Lama encouraged people to stay with the religion in which they had been raised?

The second reason I was excited was that the retreat was to be led by Jim Finley, a former monk, now turned California-based psychotherapist. Another of my key meeting-points was catered for: that between the monastic and the therapeutic. But far beyond all this, my excitement resided in the fact that Jim had, many years before, been a young monk at Gethsemani Abbey, a Trappist monastery in Kentucky, where his novice master had been Thomas Merton. It was this connection, this prospect of direct transmission from the man who, through his writings, had been my teacher since 1977 (that birthday present had been Merton's *Zen and the Birds of Appetite*) – that had brought me to be present Now, slightly elevated in the sunshine above the L.A. of 1992.

This was the Merton who had turned away from a predicted brilliant literary career (as well as an enthusiasm for women, drinking and jazz) to embrace the Roman Catholic Church and soon afterwards to enter the monastery in Kentucky where he was to live and work for 27 years until his death in 1968. There he heard and followed the growing call to solitude. Drawn to the source of all prayer via a deep connection with his earliest forerunners, the Desert Fathers and Mothers, it was Merton who seemed to have rediscovered and re-embodied the hidden practice of contemplative prayer: meditation. And it was Merton – along with others such as Bede Griffiths and John Main – who was at the very forefront of the world-changing meeting between East and West which accelerated and deepened throughout the 1960s. In 1968 the meeting became a physical reality for Merton when he was granted permission to leave the monastery and travel to Asia. His journey took in Japan, Ceylon (now Sri Lanka) and India, where he met and practised with the youthful Dalai Lama on three occasions. In Bangkok his life on earth ended because of faulty wiring in an electric fan. His last recorded words, captured on a film at the end of a talk he had just given on monasticism and Marxism, were, 'So, I will disappear from view, and we can all have a Coke or something.'

In the cool rooms of the convent Jim spoke to us from his own love of Zen, sharing some of its simple, earthy, bewildering stories about oxen, rice and monastery latrines. And he began to teach us the practice of meditation. At that time he was recommending that we keep our attention on our breath, and on nothing else, by simply counting each inhalation and exhalation as it happened, from one to ten and then starting over. I remember being struck later in the weekend by the startling courage of an American woman who asked, 'What if you don't get to two before you're distracted?' And I recall now being arrested by sudden joy and fear as Jim reminded us that, no matter how long we lived, the difference between the number of in-breaths and out-breaths in our lives would never be more than one. It was a *koan* that changed my experience of breathing for good.

Jim also taught us to sit simply, in stillness and in silence. When sensations and thought arose, to notice them and let them go. 'If you feel a real need to scratch your nose,' said Jim, 'just experiment with *not* reacting, *not* scratching your nose. Just slowing down, noticing and deciding that, after all, you don't need to scratch your nose, might just be the most important thing you've ever done in your life.' I thought I knew what Jim meant. I definitely knew what he meant when he gave us the shortest version of his teaching on meditation, just before the bell was sounded to signal that we were entering the silence and the silence was entering us: 'Just sit, and experience your own crucifixion.'

LATER

Many years later I retold this story when I was at an Easter retreat on a small island off the coast of Cork. I shared with my fellow retreatants the huge expansion that Jim's words had brought to my understanding of what we were doing – what we were participating in – when we sat to meditate. At this point a long-standing meditator from Italy (long-*sitting* is probably better) offered his response. 'That's not how it is for me at all,' he said, eyes shining with a calm joy. 'When I sit in meditation, I'm not experiencing crucifixion. I'm experiencing resurrection!'

Who's right?

Neither. And both, of course. The mysterious paradox at the heart of reality is that you can't have one without the other. All the wisdom traditions there have ever been point towards the truth that our world is being destroyed and remade moment by moment. Fullness can only come from emptiness; loss makes space for the arrival of the next unknowable gift; dispossession clears the way for an enrichment beyond our capacity to imagine – unanticipated and completely unlooked for. 'Unless a grain of wheat falls into the earth and dies, it remains just a single grain; but if it dies, it bears much fruit.'

Brahma the creator and Vishnu the sustainer would produce nothing without the joyful annihilation that Shiva brings to the dance. Theoretical physicists have been telling us the same for many years in their counter-intuitive descriptions of quantum mechanics. The languages of myth and of science offer us some truths, but in the end the only truth that transforms is the truth that we live. Being told that the crucifixion of death and the resurrection of birth aren't so different after all – in fact are inseparably intertwined – may begin our process of waking up, but it is only *information* until we consciously choose to live that truth in our fully embodied being, here and now.

Which is why some of us find ourselves meditating. In the shade of those convent rooms in California and in the Atlantic-battered retreat-house clinging to the cliffs of Ireland, we were discovering something within our individual and shared experience. With each in-breath and each out-breath we were discovering that every giving is accompanied by a letting go, a giving up. Each gift is only truly received when we are equally content to give it away. That is the simple, startling and life-changing lesson that we are all being offered as we continue to breathe. Not just, of course, if you happened to be present in the heat of California in 1992 or all those years later in the mist and spray of the Irish clifftops. But also, and always, in the very place where you choose to meditate – if you do – with others or alone, in a shrine room or a chapel, in your bedroom, in an airport terminal, on the bus, in this eternally present moment, Now.

Whether we make any 'discoveries' or learn those 'lessons' is much less important than our fully embodied *participation*. This is a far different form of discovery – it's how we come to *know with our bodies* (breathing in and breathing out) that there is no resurrection without crucifixion. And no crucifixion without resurrection. And that by opening to this ungraspable truth we can rest with equanimity in the full acceptance of Being.

Those are just words. The real meaning comes when we live it. If we choose to meditate, what we will eventually come to know, either quickly or somewhere along the faithfully (perhaps intermittently) followed path, is this: that *meditation is not what you think.*

Depression is not what you think, either. (Though in one specific and crucial sense *it is very much* what you think, as we'll see later on.)

BEYOND DESCRIPTION

Depression and meditation have some surprising territory in common. If the practice of meditation can put you in touch with an experience of agonizing surrender as well as one of astonishing freshness (crucifixion and resurrection), then there are plenty of witnesses (myself included) who will assure you that depression can also embrace the whole of that transformative mystery. It is clear, in any case, that this is what the healing force disguised as depression *wants* to do – and is capable of doing. Our task, or our invitation, is to work and play with depression so that we don't waste what it has to teach us. We have to build a relationship – perhaps what the Buddhists would call a *right* relationship – with depression. *Only connect.*

The experience of meditation and of depression both hover on the threshold of what cannot be described or even said. The ineffability of what is being experienced or what is found (if anything – and even that has to be let go of anyway) is the central theme of teachers in all the contemplative wisdom traditions. The very first lines of the *Tao Te Ching* mysteriously tell us that the name that can be spoken is not the real name, just as the way that can be followed isn't the real way. It was this very unsayability that oppressed the Buddha after his awakening. He hesitated for a long time before he was persuaded to teach. He must have felt the truth of the later Buddhist story which illustrated this conundrum with the tale of the fish asking a turtle what it was like to walk on dry land. With only the wet, the wavy and the rippling to refer to, the fish can't make head or tail of this 'dry land'. She concludes that it must be a kind of nothingness. (But it's not that either.)

It's the complaint – and the celebration – of every contemplative and mystic that the 'experience' she has had simply cannot be described. Whatever 'it' is remains stubbornly resistant to capture by language or image. It's a blessed resistance. What we encounter in the practice of meditation is a release from the limits of what can be said or represented in any other way. We are liberated into what one meditation teacher has described as 'infinite expansion'. In depression, the un-sayability of our experience has exactly the opposite quality. Here, the absence of words or images or gesture is the lock in the heavy door that keeps us in the dark – imprisoned, disconnected and mute.

In *Darkness Visible*, one of the classic accounts of depression, the celebrated American author William Styron also comes up against the frontiers of language, as we all will when we recollect or try to communicate the most deeply registered, yet most stubbornly fugitive experiences of our lives. He talks of what he went through as being 'so mysteriously painful and elusive' that it is 'close to being beyond description'. Anyone who has walked a long time with depression – and/or its non-identical twin, anxiety – will immediately recognize the truth of Styron's hard-won characterization. As soon as we try to say it, we find ourselves saying too much, or too little. We are fish talking to turtles, or turtles listening to fish.

And yet the attempt keeps on being made, as it must be. Depression – or rather the voice hidden in the depression – must find a way to say what it needs to say. Thomas Merton was a graceful and eloquent poet. 'Whether There is Enjoyment in Bitterness' is not one of his most accomplished poems, but it may be one of his bravest. Depression accompanied him both before and during his long monastic vocation. To anyone who has known the feared dark joylessness in which we are shorn of all relief, there will be something uncannily familiar in Merton's cry here:

> This afternoon, let me
> Be a sad person. Am I not
> Permitted (like other men)
> To be sick of myself?

He catalogues his overwhelming sense of hollowness, of being broken and caught in a trap of his own making, and carries on bleakly addressing an imagined, unknown listener:

> Do not forbid me (once again) to be
> Angry, bitter, disillusioned,
> Wishing I could die.

Yet Merton didn't become a contemplative simply 'to deal with' his depression. He practised the silent prayer of the heart because he found it was the best way to listen and be listened to – even through those times when it seemed that no listening at all was going on.

The trouble with trying to describe the experience of meditation as indescribable is the unavoidable implication that it is, in the end, simply another *experience* like all the other *experiences* of our day or of our life that we take possession of and catalogue. Even more misleadingly, it also suggests that there is something to be gained, some esoteric wisdom to be achieved, even a magic cure to be pulled off. But the practice is not a means to this kind of end. We all yearn for that which we can't express or describe – our mute agonies and our unspeakable joys – to be known, honoured and met in some way, without them being somehow stolen from us. There are, if we are blessed, people who can do that for, and with us. There are also animals, in the quiet glory of their non-judgemental presence, who can do it. Or wild, natural environments, or works of art that seem to know something that we didn't know we knew. Meditation, too, can become an embodied language in which we acknowledge, welcome and release that in our experience which is fearful of being captured or distorted by images and words. That's not a cure, but it *can* be a healing.

Depressed or otherwise, we are sure to find out for ourselves that meditation is not a means to an end. It is both the means *and* the end. Only practice will make that an incarnate reality, something that we truly know and understand. But if we do respond to the call of this daily practice in our lives, we might find that the bitter paralysis, the absence of communication, the agitated complexity that all writhe through Merton's poem, can be transformed in the stillness, silence and simplicity of our practice. How long will this take? One of the great twentieth-century teachers of meditation, John Main, answers this question (and many more than *just* this question) from a place of profound wisdom and psychological insight. It takes, he says, 'just as long as it takes to realize that it takes no time at all'. Another life-changing *koan*, if you hear it exactly when you are ready to hear it.

Saint Thomas Aquinas says that contemplation is 'the simple enjoyment of the truth'. That sounds wonderful. But when our current 'truth' impresses itself on us as something terrifying, overwhelming and toxic, enjoyment sounds like the least simple, and the remotest, of possibilities in our imprisoning world. Yet meditation *is* simple and – perhaps its greatest virtue – it is *simplifying*. Simple, but not easy. Nevertheless, all we have to do is begin to learn it, and keep on learning it, as beginners.

BEGINNING AGAIN

At the still point of the turning world.

The simplest and clearest description of meditation is that it is the state of being truly awake.

Or – even more accurately perhaps – the never-ending process of *choosing truly to wake up*. In committing ourselves to this practice, we agree to keep on letting go, at this very moment, of the thoughts, the daydreams and the preoccupations that shrink and control our lives. As we sit in stillness, simplicity and silence, we give the compulsions and beliefs that run our days, our minutes and our years a chance *to let go of us*. All day, every day, the internal running commentary that seems to be in charge of everything we do drags us back and forth, away from what we fear and towards what we desire. It keeps us on edge, it pulls us to the edge of our lives, sometimes to what seem like the very outskirts of life itself. In meditation we return again and again to the centre.

The centre is that place in each of us that is free of all conditions and conditioning. It is in each of us and each of us is in it. It is the peace at the heart of a reality that is constantly arising and falling away. It has been called Buddha-nature or Christ-consciousness. Jesus himself called it the *kingdom*. And he was at pains to make it clear that you can never pin it down or take possession of it, saying, *here it is* or *there it is*. All he said was that *it is in you and between you*. At the centre of everything.

Meditation is our return to, and our expression of, this shared centre. In sitting to meditate we are choosing the middle way. Not some uneasy compromise between conflicting distractions or even beliefs, but a practice that is rooted in the heart of what is. In the middle way we dispose our bodies to help us to wake up. We are neither standing nor lying down but sitting with restful attention. We are not just aware that we are breathing in or breathing out, but are gently poised at the still point of breath being given and breath being taken. We are receptive, and we are letting go of everything we receive. It all comes from, and takes us to, the centre, where there is nothing but loving, attentive wakefulness.

That is the invitation. It's up to each of us whether, and how, we respond. One of the glories of meditation is that it is free, and that we are free to do it – or not. Compulsory contemplation doesn't really work. If you're reading this book I'm assuming that you're at a point in your life when meditation (whatever you think it might be) has caught your attention, perhaps for the very first time. Or it may be that you have been meditating for years, faithfully following the teaching of a single tradition, or perhaps travelling between different forms of practice: Buddhist Vipassana, Sufi Dhikr, Quaker silence, mindfulness exercises ... And/ or you might be feeling overwhelmed, terrified or deadened by depression (whatever you think it might be), or by the thought of its return, or by your distress at its impact on someone you love.

Given all of those variables – and many more – it's good to know that meditation is not something you can get good at. If you feel yourself becoming accomplished, then you're *definitely* not good at it. The unchanging gift at the heart of this practice is one that will always gently and lovingly outwit the games that the mind wants to play. Especially the mind that is relentlessly down on itself in the crush of criticism out of which depression is made. 'I can't do it', 'I'm not good enough', 'I'm too stupid', 'I'm bound to mess it up', 'Everyone else is going to be better at this than me' – the destructive mantras of our everyday thoughts are endless. But these are the very thoughts that meditation disarmingly welcomes (and some version of them *will* always occur). Unless they are first acknowledged and welcomed, we won't be able to let them go as they keep on returning. The essence of meditation is not to succeed but to steadfastly return to the simplicity of the practice, time and time again after every one of our self-described failures (and successes). It's a way of learning to keep ourselves open to the presence of effortless forgiveness – the true work of love. In meditation we cannot fail to be good enough.

Whether we are 'experienced' meditators or not, and whatever state of mind we might be dealing with, it is *always* time to begin again. Depression will argue against that, being the very embodiment of everything that wants to oppose this truth. Locked in that state of being, we can feel overwhelmed by the crushing illusion that there will never be another beginning, nothing will ever be new, because everything has come to a full stop. And there *will* be times when we are incapable of practising meditation, just as we might be temporarily overcome by the impossibility of going for a run, meeting a friend or even getting out of bed. Nevertheless, the practice itself is infinitely patient. It will wait for us. When we are ready (and sometimes we are surprised to find that we are ready before we *feel* ready), we can begin, or begin again, to meditate. It is our opportunity to join in with the truth (which has no opposite) simply expressed by the Zen insight that *everything is always just beginning*.

HOW TO MEDITATE

If you already follow a meditation practice, then continue with that practice. But take this opportunity, and every opportunity, to remind yourself that – actually – you have never done this before. Meditation is not a cosy pair of slippers or a familiar shawl that we can put on to comfortably daydream the time away. We are giving our attention as fully as we can to being awake, to what is always new, no matter how many hundreds or thousands of times we have 'done it' before. Perhaps it never truly begins until 'we' stop 'doing it'. Maybe we can best think of our meditation as simply *joining in*.

There are a few simple universal teachings about how to join in. I offer them here along with the recommendation of a mantra – a prayer word – that can be the focus of your meditation. In many traditions it is the awareness of the breath itself that is the essence of the practice. We'll explore the mantra further later on. For now you can just decide for yourself whether to use it or simply to stay with the breath as the object of your attention:

- Find a quiet and comfortable place to sit. If you can find or create a space in your home which you can designate as your regular place of meditation, that can be helpful. If you want, place images or objects there that you love, that you know, to support you in your practice.

- Meditating on a chair is fine, but preferably not one that is soft and designed for TV-watching or falling asleep. A meditation stool or cushion is good too.
- If you're sitting on a chair, make sure your feet are flat on the ground and that you have a good firm contact with whatever is under your feet.
- Sit with an alert but relaxed posture. Above all, sit with your back straight. Not as though it's some kind of military discipline, but to gently allow the energy in your being to flow freely, perhaps for the first time in hours … in days … in years …
- Before you begin the period of meditation, bring your awareness to your body; to the places that are hurting or where tension is being held (it might even feel that this is the whole of your body). Notice it and offer as much acceptance, forgiveness and compassion to your body as you are able to. Welcome this guest, your faithful body, which has been breathing in and out for as long as you can remember. Allow it to carry on doing that with your full cooperation, your newly opening awareness.
- Don't hurry any of this.
- Let your attention rest on your breath. Notice that it's not just *your* breath. It arrives and it leaves, arrives and leaves, over and over again. Allow all of your attention to ride with your breath as you receive it and gently give it away.

- There is no need to do anything to consciously alter your breathing. Merely bringing your awareness to it will tend to slow it and allow it to be felt lower down in your body, towards your belly. (When we are tense and anxious and our attention is scattered, we tend to have shallow, rapid breathing, involving only the upper part of the chest.)
- As you settle gradually into the stillness, simplicity and silence of your breathing, begin the interior reciting of your prayer word or phrase. Allow it to sound within you, perhaps like the deep, steady chiming of a bell. Listen to it, give your whole attention to it. You might have a particular sacred word or phrase that has a special resonance for you – by all means use that. There is also great power in using a word that is initially unfamiliar, that you don't even know the meaning of. The word I'm going to recommend is from the ancient Aramaic language: *maranatha*. Four equally stressed syllables: *ma-ra-na-tha*. Its 'meaning' is the least important thing about it at this moment. To take this word for the very first time as the entire focus of your being during the period of meditation is an act of trusting innocence – as it will be on the thousandth time you do it. Just how the mantra works is something to be further explored later on; for now, experience really is the only teacher.
- Say the word silently and listen to it faithfully throughout the period of meditation. Hearing it further down in your body (and not just somewhere between your ears) is something that you might notice or experiment with. As with the breathing,

the movement in meditation is from the head to the heart.

- Twenty minutes might be a good length of time to start with. If you feel you can only manage ten minutes, or even only five at this stage, that's fine too.

- When you find yourself thinking about things other than the mantra (as you always will – sometimes it will feel like ALL the time), gently bring your attention back to the home of the breath or the mantra. Carry on doing this from the beginning until the end of the meditation period, safe in the knowledge that this is the way of being where there are no mistakes and no failures. You are simply waking up. *Maranatha, ma-ra-na-tha.*

Meditate for 20 minutes

After meditation:

Except for the point, the still point, There would be no dance, and there is only the dance.

T. S. Eliot

MEDITATION *AND* DEPRESSIONS

Father Richard Rohr is a Franciscan friar and priest who lives in New Mexico. In 1986 he set up the Center for Action and Contemplation in Albuquerque. Over the years he reports that some people have found themselves slightly puzzled by the two words in the Center's title, which they somehow don't expect to see together. *Action* and *Contemplation*. How do they fit? And (perhaps being people whose dualistic approach makes them feel more comfortable when they have tidied these things up) they have apparently often asked Father Richard which is the most important word in the Center's title. He has always gloried in answering with a resounding 'AND!'

It feels the same to me with Meditation and Depressions. It's not simply a matter of what one looks like from the perspective of the other. That would be just another outbreak of dualistic tidiness. It's much more about *living through* the intimate relationship that they share, and so changing in a profound way the experience and the understanding that we have of both.

When I was invited to write a book on the theme of meditation and depression, one of my initial concerns was about authenticity. I had first practised meditation nearly forty years beforehand. So I had done enough to know that I knew very little about meditation except that you can't get good at it. I had also had a number of periods in my life when I had felt severely hampered – and, on a blessedly few occasions, overwhelmed and terrified – by experiences that, for shorthand, I had agreed to describe to myself and the world as *depression* and *anxiety*. Somehow, none of these episodes had led to me being hospitalized, or even using any of the mental health services – statutory or voluntary – that were on offer. I did once sit awkwardly and hesitantly with a very understanding and sympathetic GP, trying to describe my plight, and explaining why, no matter how bad I felt, I was convinced that antidepressants were not for me. (They *are* for some people, and do seem to have been helpful according to many personal accounts. How *my* times of crippling anguish turned into a pilgrimage of recovery is quite clear to me. That pilgrim way was a blessed interweaving of many paths. We'll look carefully at medication, treatment and recovery in a vital later section.)

My concern was this: I had spent a lot of time practising doing nothing, in a good way (meditation), and was certainly no stranger to feeling like less than nothing, in a very, very bad way (depression and anxiety). But for quite a number of years I had felt a degree of ... what to call it ... *balance, equilibrium, equanimity*? What about a much underused and undervalued word – *sanity*? Certainly, for a long time I hadn't experienced the grinding, moment-by-moment, world-cancelling agony which people who know depression and anxiety will be familiar with. That being the case, the faint worry at the back of my mind was whether I would be able to do justice to the state of being that is associated with depression. Was I going to be writing this book as a meditator trying valiantly to remember what it was like to be depressed? Would I just be reproducing some rather anodyne simulacrum of that appalling confrontation with your own existence and non-existence? Was I inevitably going to betray the experience and all the people who have gone through it, who are going through it and who will go through it? There is a Spanish proverb which summed up my dilemma beautifully: *No es lo mismo hablar de toros que estar en el redondel* (It is not the same thing to talk of bulls as to be in the bullring). I needn't have worried. The bulls and I were about to be released into the same arena.

***

About a year before, I had experienced a sudden shocking loss. My hearing. I woke up one morning to find that I couldn't hear anything through my right ear. Except an insistent and very loud noise, as if a large steam engine was panting and wheezing with monotonous regularity right next to my head. While a gale was blowing. I was eventually diagnosed with sudden sensorineural hearing loss, which is the kind that is nearly always permanent. The hissing and whooshing that had taken the place of the familiar sounds of the world – birds singing, the clatter of supermarket trolleys, some gentle words murmured in my ear – this was the *tinnitus* associated with some instances of hearing loss. 'Phantom' sounds that are experienced as overwhelmingly real by the baffled listener. The loss (and the unwanted gain of the tinnitus) felt like a catastrophe. How was I going to manage to communicate effectively? How could I cope with social situations – noisy pubs, the cacophony of railway stations, even the excited chatter of conversation before and after silent retreats? How could I read, write, sing, walk, converse, eat, play badminton, meditate …? How could I live?

I was blessed with sympathetic and supportive doctors and audiologists. Friends and family were understanding and unwavering. I went away on holiday, came back and slowly discovered that, actually, I could still do all of those things, with a few adjustments, mainly of my own expectations. The other great healer was that old favourite, time. *Habituation* is the good friend of the tinnitus sufferer – perhaps of everyone who has lost something precious or acquired something profoundly undesired. Where hearing is concerned, the brain, with its built-in and enduring plasticity, is stupendously adept at adjusting to new conditions. It adapts to the change, recognizes new norms and sets its defaults accordingly. Within a few months my 'unilateral hearing loss' had diminished to a fairly major inconvenience, but one that could certainly be lived with. The tinnitus, when I noticed it, had hushed to a gentle susurration which at times I experienced as almost comfortingly familiar. And I still had one fully functional ear left. The bulls had been quickly rounded up and put safely back in their pens. I had scarcely had a chance to get a good look at them.

But if I wanted to get to know them better – again, there was no need for me to worry. A few months further down the line some sympathetically offered treatment in a hospital ENT department had the unintended consequence of waking the quiescent tinnitus. The steam engine started up again. The gale revived. And now it was all happening next to the constant crashing of waves against the shore. Plus someone had turned it all up to maximum volume. There were also a few extra features thrown in to my new hearing environment. Suddenly I was acutely aware of loud noises; and noises that hadn't seemed loud before (cutlery on a plate, water from the tap, the crinkling of a plastic bag) were now exploding uncomfortably somewhere in my head. And when I heard speech – most distressingly of all, my own voice – it was as if someone was crashing cymbals together in time with each word. Once more I went away on holiday, only this time it seemed that habituation wasn't ready to do its healing work.

A few months down the line and the symptoms seemed to be unchanged. The relentless inescapability of it all began to weigh heavily on me. I started to feel more and more compromised, increasingly averse to situations where I was expected to talk or listen (pretty much every social encounter), and gradually started to disconnect. Nothing felt familiar, least of all myself – everything was becoming strange and threatening. Before long I was having sensations that I dimly recognized. My limbs began to feel heavy and painful. My mouth was consistently dry. My head felt foggy, my eyes ready to close at all times. I began to crave the refuge of my bed and the night, when I could at least allow the aching question mark that my body had become to curl up in some kind of foetal safety.

The bed-time asylum though – like everything else – was double-edged. It did afford me a kind of regressed trance where I could cut off from all demands and threats. But it would also relentlessly deliver me to the morning with its starkly unchanged rush of impossibilities. On waking from my protective stupor, there would be the ongoing horror of finding that I still felt – from moment to moment – either encased in lead or made entirely of glass, and often both. Sometimes the slow-motion drugged feeling would be quickly replaced by the slide of a much more vicious dread. Something in my belly would tighten, my breath would become shallow and a panicky fizzing would start beating in my chest and my throat. A nameless fear threatened to swamp everything. Whatever was going on, and whatever I was doing, an unvoiced question attached itself to every activity and gesture, no matter how trivial: *What's the point? What's the point? What's the point?* I was in control of nothing and everything was in control of me. Eventually, despite my resistance, I found myself giving this whole set of experiences a name. I called it *depression*. And all the time the roar in my almost-dead ear carried on rhythmically and insistently. It had begun to sound like the crazed breathing of a maddened beast. I knew what it was. The bulls were very, very close again.

WEARY, STALE, FLAT

The worst thing about experiences like this is that you feel utterly alone. Nobody else, you are convinced, is going through this, and nobody else ever has – or will. This entrenched belief, of course, is itself what keeps us isolated. The irony is that there are numberless accounts of such experiences in literature, memoir, myth, history and – now – in the seething universal library that is the internet. Stories of emotional paralysis and despair are everywhere on YouTube, on blogs and on TV celebrity chat-couches. Sometimes it helps to hear these testimonies. *Perhaps I'm not so alone, not so strange after all?* At other times the conviction about the uniqueness of your own despair is overwhelming. The stories of recovery serve only to separate you even further from any hope of being spared. *They're alright now – but I'm a special case, there's no way back for* **me**.

It's nothing new. Something like this kind of hopeless anguish seems to have accompanied human beings always. Certainly for as long as they have been able to attempt some kind of record of what they have been going through. As far back as we are able to listen, we hear the voice of the lost and broken self:

> And now my life ebbs away; days of suffering grip me.
> Night pierces my bones; my gnawing pains never rest.

This is Job, whose story is told in the book of the Old Testament that bears his name. He is a wealthy man, living in peaceful harmony, surrounded by family and all the good things that have rewarded his sound stewardship. At a stroke, he loses all of his possessions, all of his children, all of his servants. There is nothing left. Then he is afflicted with 'loathsome sores' all over his body. His health has gone too. Adrift now in endless misery, he wishes that he had never been born. Life is dreadful and impossible:

> For the thing which I greatly feared is come upon me, and that which I was afraid of is come unto me. I was not in safety, neither had I rest, neither was I quiet; yet trouble came.

He doesn't spare the harsh practical details. His once dependable body is in chaos and his place in society is utterly changed:

My inward parts are in turmoil and are never still; days of
affliction come to meet me. I go about in sunless gloom;
I stand up in the assembly and cry for help.

Some translations render 'inward parts' as 'heart', others
as the much more visceral 'bowels'. No part of his being is
functioning or at peace.

In the very next book of the Old Testament – Psalms –
we hear the groans, and sometimes the howls, of a voice
crying from what sounds like the same place:

Many bulls have compassed me:
strong bulls of Bashan have beset me round.
They gaped upon me with their mouths,
as a ravening and a roaring lion.
I am poured out like water,
and all my bones are out of joint:
my heart is like wax; it is melted in the midst of my
    bowels.
My strength is dried up like a potsherd;
and my tongue cleaveth to my jaws;
and thou hast brought me into the dust of death.

The description – especially in these words of the King
James Bible – is even more vivid, more searingly lyrical than
the complaints of Job. This is clearly an existential crisis –
a malaise of the spirit, the mind and the heart, but it is
also insistently and overwhelmingly a *physical* experience,
penetrating every part of the suffering body. (And there are
the bulls again, getting even closer.)

The same note of abject hopelessness sounds like
a cracked bell throughout the Psalms, against the

background of all the other jostling moods: praise, rage, envy, joy, bafflement. Psalm 38 sums up the zero point of despair:

> I am troubled; I am bowed down greatly;
> I go mourning all the day long.
> For my loins are filled with a loathsome disease:
> and there is no soundness in my flesh.
> I am feeble and sore broken: .
> I have roared by reason of the disquietness of my heart.

Variations of this state, and of the fractured attempts to give it voice or shape, echo throughout the subsequent histories, myths and memoirs of our collective story. And so we meet the Fisher King of Celtic and Arthurian myth. Condemned by a mysterious but utterly debilitating wound, he is condemned to live out his life surrounded by the dying wasteland that his frozen kingdom has become. His internal devastation is so complete that it has spilled over and infected the whole of his world. Helpless, hopeless and impotent, he is too ill to live but not ill enough to die. His only relief comes from the silent and solitary fishing with which he passes his pointless time on the earth.

And then there's Hamlet, caught in the mirror held unwaveringly up to nature. The first – and perhaps still the fullest – attempt by humanity to show itself to itself in all of its psychological complexity. He seems to be adrift in a version of the Fisher King's blasted and inhospitable territory:

> I have of late – but wherefore I know not – lost all my
> mirth, forgone all custom of exercises, and indeed it goes

so heavily with my disposition that this goodly frame,
the earth, seems to me a sterile promontory ...

He, too, does what he can to talk about, and from, this place
where there is no hope, no pleasure and just the desperate
wish for it all to be over:

> O that this too too sullied flesh would melt,
> Thaw and resolve itself into a dew,
> Or that the Everlasting had not fix'd
> His canon 'gainst self-slaughter! O God, God!
> How weary, stale, flat, and unprofitable
> Seem to me all the uses of this world!

Here is the first truly modern person speaking to himself
and to us. He may not be historical, but he certainly feels
real, and what he's struggling to say is really familiar.

Closer to us in time, and unarguably real, is one of
Hamlet's celebrated readers and editors, Dr Samuel Johnson.
In popular imagination he stands solidly for the entire, and
entirely reasonable, matter-of-fact eighteenth century, but
his life was shot through with long periods of intense and
debilitating misery. He describes himself as:

> broken off from mankind; a kind of solitary wanderer in the
> wild of life, without any direction or fixed point of view: a
> gloomy gazer on the world to which I have little relation.

In verse he manages to be more specific and even more
painfully physical:

> The listless will succeeds, that worst disease,
> The rack of indolence, the sluggish ease.

Care grows on care, and o'er my aching brain
Black melancholy pours her morbid train.

Whatever this experience is, it's a kind of torture. It hurts like Hell, and in places that you don't seem able to touch.

Wherever we look in the records of the human race we can find this state of dejected paralysis. Something about it seems to be universal. It is there, front and centre, at the very beginning of the great foundational text of Eastern religion and philosophy, 'India's greatest gift to the world', the *Bhagavad Gita*. Written perhaps just a little later than the Book of Job (and certainly much later than the most ancient of the Psalms), the *Gita* opens with the drama of enormous forces facing each other on a battlefield. Something huge and terrifying is about to begin. The warrior-hero Arjuna surveys the scene. The pointlessness and the absurdity of the situation suddenly overwhelms him. He's not frightened of dying or being injured; it's just that none of it makes sense to him any more. He doesn't want to kill, he doesn't want to destroy – in short, he wants no part of what lies in front of him. He turns to his guide and charioteer, Lord Krishna, and describes what he's experiencing:

My limbs sink down
And my mouth becomes parched,
And there is trembling in my body
And my hair stands on end.

My bow falls from my hand,
And my skin too is burning,
And I cannot stand still,
And my mind seems to wander.

He ends up declaring that it would be better if he was dead. This opening chapter of the *Gita* is called 'Arjuna Vishada Yoga'. 'Vishada' has been variously translated throughout the centuries as *sorrow, grief, sadness, despair, despondency*. The most common translation is *dejection*. In Sanskrit, *yoga* can mean not just a spiritual practice or a way of living, but also a state of mind or a condition. So we can call this opening chapter 'Arjuna's State of Dejection'. One of the great wisdom teachings seems to take as a given that the beginning of true self-knowledge lies in this condition where you are paralysed, fearful and ready to give up.

Arjuna, of course, is not *just* a prince, a hero and a warrior of myth from a far distant time and culture. He stands in for all of us. He is the suddenly terrified human being, contemplating the world that he or she is supposed to take part in, feeling (like Hamlet) the impossibility of taking any action, and only capable of registering weakness, fear and futility.

> Thus spoke Arjuna in the field of battle,
> And letting fall his bow and arrows
> He sank down in his chariot,
> His soul overcome by despair and grief.

It's significant that all of these everypersons – Job, David, the Fisher King, Hamlet, Dr Johnson, Arjuna – have been every*men*. The famous line has it that 'history is written by the victors'. Even, apparently, the history of experiences that seem to speak of failure, loss and defeat. For too long, men appointed themselves as the *de facto* victors in everything. They became the producers and the keepers of all the records. It's not that women haven't suffered in this way.

Of course they have. And a large part of the mental and emotional suffering – the depressions – of women through the ages has come from this ordering of things. Women's experiences just didn't count for as much as men's. That's why it has taken so long to hear women's voices. It's a silencing which has added to sufferings that were already nearly impossible to express. So it's good and just that the last of our everypersons in this section is a contemporary and profoundly articulate woman.

Gwyneth Lewis is a poet. She has also been a journalist and documentary producer. Appointed as the very first National Poet of Wales in 2005, hers are the giant words that hang over the Millennium Centre in Cardiff: *IN THESE STONES HORIZONS SING …*

Gwyneth has also written an account of her own experiences of mental and emotional collapse in a book she called *Sunbathing in the Rain: A Cheerful Book on Depression*. Dorothy Rowe – a writer and psychologist who has done more than anyone over the past few decades to change our response to these episodes of bleak despair – has described it as 'undoubtedly the best book I have ever read about one person's experience of depression'. The book opens with Gwyneth declaring that 'Every serious episode of depression is a murder mystery.' So, of course, she wants to know

What happened? Who killed me?
In less than a week I'd gone from being a person who cared about clothes, being out in the world, writing, food, to being a wreck who cowered from everything.

She takes to her bed:

Under the duvet, an internal ice age had set in. I had permafrost around my heart. This is what dying of cold must be like, once the numbness has started.

Just as in all the other accounts, there is no part of her suffering flesh that doesn't register the agony:

Imagine feeling sick, not only in your stomach but throughout every part of your body – your arms, your cheeks, even the palms of your hands, a bit like sea-sickness but the more virulent for being less physical.

Rereading her account, I found myself nodding in recognition, and I imagined Job and David and all the others – if they were for a moment able to lift their heads – doing just the same. And I dare to guess that you, reading this now, if you've had some taste of something like these experiences, will be resonating with all these brave attempts to say just what it was like. It provokes a kind of muscle memory of our own time of prostration, which may be just behind us, distantly remembered or still stubbornly filling our days. It's troubling, but it can also be encouraging. For here is a woman whose sense of purpose, meaning and physical capacity to do anything has suddenly collapsed (just like Arjuna's). But – like Arjuna – against all the odds and all expectations, it turns out to be for her the beginning of a profound transformation. That's why one of the key messages in *Sunbathing in the Rain* is this: 'The last thing you should do is waste your depression. Please don't let all that suffering go to waste.'

There's one more parallel with the struggling hero of the *Bhagavad Gita* (who is encouraged by Lord Krishna to follow the way of contemplation): during her recovery, our Welsh poet deepened into a practice of Zen meditation as the rain fell and the permafrost slowly melted.

***

It's tempting to look at all these accounts of debilitating anguish and come to the glib conclusion that there is a universal experience that men and women have always been prey to. That throughout the ages, the mind, body and spirit of a person can be flattened and broken, sometimes for apparently obvious reasons, sometimes more mysteriously. That, however it comes about, there is this given phenomenon and the only thing that changes is the language that we couch it in, the name that we give it. Of all the testimonies that we've listened to here, only Gwyneth Lewis's uses the word 'depression' to talk about what is going on. There's a simple reason for that – the word was just not available in other cultures and at other times. The closest would be Dr Johnson and his contemporaries, who could certainly talk of 'a depression of spirits'. Yet the idea of 'depression' itself as an illness, disease, experience, cultural fact or even something to write a book about, simply didn't exist.

The extreme version of the 'universalizing' conclusion – that women and men have always gone through these more or less unchanging experiences – would go on to celebrate the fact that, at last, we've found the right name for it. Depression has finally been properly identified as ... depression. Such a conclusion, as well as being rather obviously circular, somehow fails to pay the kind of respectful attention that such profound human struggles demand. In the face of the sufferings of our fellow beings – our other selves – the compassionate response is simply to *listen* as deeply as we can, having suspended all the categories, ideas and beliefs that we are usually only too ready to bundle life up in. To be, in other words, less diagnostic.

If we are able to pay the right kind of attention to the person in front of us, and to our own shifting experiences, we will learn to have a lighter touch with our language. The urgent lesson that then emerges for our own healing and the healing of others is this: *it matters a great deal what name we choose to give things*. And so the important questions follow, ones that you might never have put to yourself, but questions that suffering makes it vital for each of us to consider: is the very word *depression* imprisoning us or setting us free? What does it do when we give something a name? What happens when we change it? And what happens in those moments of clarity, when we give up altogether on stories and names?

Put those questions – and everything else – aside for the moment: it's time to meditate again.

MEDITATION: NOTHING TO BE DONE

At its worst, in the depths, we can end up feeling that we have become nothing. Where once there was a person, a familiar self that we recognized and were ready to share with others, there is now an emptiness. My sense of who I am has shrunk down to a vanishing point whose location is completely unknown. Somehow I have wandered – or fallen – into something like the desert that the wisdom teachers encourage us to know, to explore and to make our lasting home. Only they call it Heaven, and this feels like Hell. *What new madness is this?*

Our way through this territory lies in a completely different understanding of both *Nothing* and *Emptiness*.

In meditation we practise the letting go of the *thing-ness* of our lives. The objects, the stories and the possessions – mental, emotional and spiritual – with which we forge an identity. These are the things that come to define us. In the end the most essential of our possessions is a familiar and (usually) well-defended sense of self. Some, for shorthand, call it the ego. When we meditate we are loosening our identification with all these self-creating things, by choosing to place our attention elsewhere. It's a process of voluntary emptying. In doing this we are following the way of Jesus who 'became as nothing', choosing the mysterious path of surrendering his own will. We are also entering into the boundless field of *sunyata*, the 'empty' reality that the Buddha pointed towards, where all beings and all phenomena give rise to each other in an endless dance of co-creation. This *nothing* and this *emptiness* are not concerned with the heroic seduction of self-punishment, non-existence and annihilation. They are the supreme affirmation that our deepest identity lies not in the separateness of *things*, but in the dynamic flow that connects all of life.

At some point in my practice of meditation I came to understand it as the practice of *no-thing*, where the word functions just like the word *breathing*. Grammatically speaking, it becomes a participle. As I sit, I am *no-thing* myself, the world and everything that arises in it. I am recognizing it all as, and allowing it all to be, *no thing*. I am doing this by taking possession of none of it, as it arises and falls away, breath by breath. If I allow myself and everything that arises in my consciousness to be *no thing*, then life is instantaneously completely present, in all of its radiant abundance and fullness.

'Nothing to be done' are the first words of Samuel Beckett's masterpiece, *Waiting for Godot*. After its first performance one critic described it as a play 'in which nothing happens, twice'. A witty summary of a brilliant work. But in meditation we can discover that *no-thing* is actually something that we *can* do. There really is *no-thing* to be done. And we are the ones to do it, sitting on our chair or our cushion, alone or with our fellow meditators. All we have to dare is to be 'empty' of things and to do 'nothing'.

When we are depressed, we feel at our most thing-like. We have been overtaken by this thing called *depression*. We feel not like a living being, but more like an object. We are in the possession of thoughts and beliefs about ourselves which clutter and impede the flow of our lives. Things have got on top of us. If we are able, for just a few moments, to be not quite so fiercely attached to the jumble of clashing objects that fill our heads and cramp our bodies, then we have a chance to find something that is always new and always alive. Or, even more thrillingly, to be found. By what? By that which will never objectify you, never turn you into a thing.

One of my favourite ways of understanding this profound shift from life as thing-ness to life as vital, connective movement is by thinking of nouns and verbs. Nouns are the word-things that we use to cut the world up into separate building-blocks. They are static and fixed. Verbs are the living energy that run like quicksilver through and between all 'things'. If we could see clearly enough, we would know that, in truth, there are only verbs, and that nouns are a necessary fiction. Matter is simply spirit moving slowly enough to be seen, as Teilhard de Chardin wonderfully described it. In meditation we sit with the willingness to move from being nouns to becoming verbs, to shift away from fixity back into the flow of life.

Before meditation:

A condition of complete simplicity
(Costing not less than everything)

T. S. Eliot

Meditate for 20 minutes

After meditation:

There is a Spirit which is mind and life, light and truth and
vast spaces. He contains all things, all works and desires and
all perfumes and tastes. And he enfolds the whole universe and,
in silence, is loving to all. This is the Spirit that is in my heart,
smaller than a grain of rice, or a grain of barley, or a grain of
mustard-seed or a grain of canary-seed, or the kernel of a grain
of canary-seed. This is the Spirit that is in my heart, greater than
the earth, greater than the sky, greater than heaven itself, greater
than all these worlds. This is the Spirit that is in my heart.

From the *Chandogya Upanishad*

BY ANY OTHER NAME

In Ursula Le Guin's short story 'The Rule of Names', the central character (a slightly incompetent wizard) makes an announcement that 'The name is the thing, and the true name is the true thing. To speak the name is to control the thing.' The whole of this little fable takes place in an imaginary land where children are given a provisional name, which is then replaced by a 'true name' as they reach adulthood. This new name must be kept secret though, as it contains and reflects the very essence of the named person. To carelessly reveal it would risk putting yourself in the power of others. The True Name has supreme value; it is sacred.

The story plays with the idea that 'naming magic' is at work, not just in the realm of myth and fantasy, but throughout our real lives, in our real world. The power of naming lies at the beginning of all the stories of beginnings – the world's great creation myths. In Genesis, God seems to name into existence everything that is: 'And God said, Let there be light: and there was light.' God carries on in this way until he makes all the living creatures from out of the ground, after which he proceeds to create the first man. But at this point he holds back and brings all the creatures to Adam. In an act of what seems like co-creation, Adam is invited by God to name all these birds of the air and animals of the field. 'And whatever the man called every living creature, that was its name.' In an ancient Egyptian creation myth, the deity *Ptah* is much less cooperative. He undertakes the whole thing without any help from anybody else. And in his myth, the act of naming is even more central. He brings all things into being simply by thinking of them and then saying their names with his tongue.

Naming has a terrible power. It can be seen as akin to creation. If you name something, it is as if you make it. Even more – it's as if you *make it your own*. Naming rights bring with them the possibility of possession and control. No wonder that the naming of God has always been the most sensitive of subjects. Who has the right to take possession or control of God? Even by using the word *God*? The wisdom of both the Islamic and the Judaic traditions veers away from this trap, set at the very heart of naming. Islam celebrates the infinite abundance of the Supreme Being by listing the 99 names of God. The symbolically enormous number seems to point to the truth that there is no end to the naming that is appropriate in the face of such limitless mercy and grace. Judaism places the emphasis on the awful sacredness of the one true name. So potent and immeasurable is it that it could only be said on the rarest of occasions and under very specific conditions. Beyond that, it is best to refrain from naming God at all.

Both responses (extravagantly over-naming on the one hand, prohibition on the other) express a fundamental anxiety about naming. (God, of course, is a special case. The only thing worse than giving God a false name, is speaking God's true name.) This anxiety, though, is not just about naming God, but about naming everything. It's been a central concern of philosophers and poets and contemplatives through the ages. Socrates started it off by wondering whether names are 'conventional' or 'natural'. In other words, is a name just an arbitrary sign or does it uniquely speak the very essence and identity of the thing named? The same question hangs in the air at that heart-stopping moment when a child or an adult is suddenly in wonder and asks for the first time: *what's the difference between the thing and what we call the thing?* There's the table. And there's *the table.* There's love. And there's the word *love.* How can we separate them? Is there a difference? And what happens if we call it something else? Or if we go with Alice through the looking-glass and into the forest where all things lose their names?

It seems to me that if we're wanting (no matter how fitfully) to wake up, then we can put this creative anxiety – about things and the names we give them – to good use. What if we decide to do some naming magic of our own? If it *is* the case that knowing the true name of someone or something gives you control over him or it, then what does it mean if we persist in calling something by the wrong name? Are we then in the grip of somebody else's naming magic? Are we giving away the power and the control that are rightfully ours? Aiming for the True Name of everything right away might be a bit over-ambitious. But beginning to find some *truer* names will be a very promising start.

THE INVENTION OF DEPRESSION

> What shall we think of a people who ... for depression,
> used the word that described the vulnerable phase in
> a crab's seasonal cycle, when it has sloughed off its old
> shell and waits for another to grow?

These are the words of Bruce Chatwin from his classic 1977 work of travel writing, *In Patagonia*. His journeying through the wild lands at the tip of South America have brought him into contact with the descendants of a nineteenth-century missionary called Thomas Bridges. One of Bridges' achievements was the compilation of a dictionary that records the words of the 'primitive' *Yámana* people, who had lived in these lands since long before the arrival of modern colonists. As Chatwin pores over the monumental work of scholarship, he marvels at the vivid nature of the indigenous people's language, rooted in animal life and natural phenomena. What the Victorian missionary and linguist thought of these people, it's difficult to know. He may well have judged the speech of the 'Indian natives' to be rudimentary – lacking in the medical, scientific and moral concepts that a high-minded nineteenth-century European found so essential.

For us though, like Chatwin, it's difficult not to be struck by the painful vividness of that image: the soft, white, unprotected body of the crab; its reflexive anxiety as it moves from one necessary stage of its life to the next; the utter powerlessness in these long moments of precarious transformation; the instinct of hope that speaks of a bigger and better protection, that tells it to wait. What *are* we to think of these people who had this word and these ideas?

What would it be like if everyone in your culture thought of 'depression' in those terms? Wouldn't it make a difference to how we understood it in relation to the rest of our lives? And wouldn't it have profound implications for how we respond to it and how we treat each other?

I wish I knew what the actual *Yámana* word was for *depression/that moment in a crab's life*. Perhaps at some point in the future a visit to the British Museum (where Bridges' original manuscript is housed) will reveal it to me. For now, it stands as a mysteriously invisible reminder that our words and descriptions are always provisional. Our ideas about things determine what we call them. And the names that we give them in turn influence our ideas. And so it goes around, with our understanding of depressions and crustaceans and everything else under the sun shifting and evolving, sometimes in sudden surges, sometimes in slow sideways movements – like a crab. Every age, and every culture, of course, believes that *its* words and *its* ideas are the ones closest to the truth. But who is to say? Is it more truthful to describe an experience as a moment of understandable vulnerability in a creature's life, or as a disease?

To begin to respond fully to a question like that we need to be able to take a step back from the 'self-evident' assumptions that our culture urges on us all the time. There are things that we are asked to take for granted, simply because we are alive at this time, and because we are all in this together. It's all too easy to forget that our collective and individual reality is something constructed in *this* particular culture at *this* particular point in history. 'He not busy being born is busy dying', sings Bob Dylan. If we're not trying to wake up, we can spend most of our time in the deathly grip of received wisdom. 'Depression is depression' would be the common-sense contemporary slogan (just as, at the time of writing, 'Brexit means Brexit'). But depression hasn't always been *depression*. Beginning to understand what that means doesn't simply bring a theoretical or academic satisfaction. It can be the first vital step that you take, or help others to take, in the gentle pilgrimage of recovery.

***

The most startling piece of information for many people living in what seems like a depression-saturated twenty-first century is that 50 years ago depression as we conceive of it was hardly known. In 1950 it was estimated that only 0.5 per cent of the population of the United States was affected. Now – in 2018 – the World Health Organization (WHO) declares that 'depression is the leading cause of ill health and disability worldwide'. It has predicted that it will affect between 25 and 45 per cent of the global adult population, with a recorded increase of 18 per cent between 2005 and 2015 alone. WHO figures for 2017 estimate that 300 million people worldwide 'are now living with depression'. In the United States nearly one in four middle-aged women are currently taking antidepressants. In the UK the number of annual prescriptions for depression rose between 2006 and 2016 by 108.5 per cent to 65 million. The obvious and urgent question for those of us who think of ourselves as depressed, or who have been diagnosed as such, is: what has been happening since 1950? And what was happening before? A historical perspective will cast some light into our present moment.

Nearly two and a half thousand years ago, Hippocrates and his followers would have understood a fellow Greek's miserable suffering as a result of a humoral imbalance. Four distinct bodily fluids were the vital constituent parts of each person: yellow bile, phlegm, blood and black bile. Each of these humours had its seat in a particular organ of the body and gave rise to identifiable behaviours and temperaments. Maintaining the balance between them was the key to health and sanity. A preponderance of black bile (*melaina chole*), rising from the spleen and the bowel, would result in an experience of anguish, guilt, loss of purpose, self-loathing and social withdrawal – something that we might recognize as *melancholy*.

This humoral understanding of physical and mental wellbeing was taken forward by Galen (as the Roman superpower replaced the Greek), refined by Arab medicine and then built on by the insights of the Renaissance and the Enlightenment. It remained the predominant model of health until well into the nineteenth century. Someone whose life was blighted by dejection and a crippling absence of vitality might be described variously as *melancholic, hypochondriack* or perhaps as suffering *from an excess of the spleen*. The condition even became synonymous with national identity – one eighteenth-century writer reported that 'By Foreigners ... nervous Distempers, Spleen, Vapours, and Lowness of Spirits, are, in Derision, called the English Malady.'

But the English didn't have a monopoly on low spirits and stalled lives. As the medical profession grew into a newly 'scientific' confidence and a sense of its own burgeoning power, the next generation of words to describe bewildering human anguish were generated in North America, France, Germany, Vienna ... As the nineteenth century drew to a close, *neurasthenia, fatigue, hysteria, anxiety* and *neurosis* were now the kind of terms used to designate what seemed to be happening in lives that had become joyless and turned in on themselves. The new language signalled the inexorably gathering momentum in the profession of medicine. The discovery of bacteria and the invention of bacteriology from the 1880s onwards permanently shifted the way that doctors thought and worked. The humoral theory died a rapid death as the medical gaze switched to dysfunctions of specific organs and systems. The emphasis was now on the *parts* of the body and the mind, and what could go wrong with them – the newly 'discovered' diseases.

Whatever we might think of the theory of the four humours and the real or imagined bodily fluids that coursed through human bodies and history for so many centuries, one thing that we can say about the approach is that it was holistic. It attempted to look at whole people, at their diet, their activities, how they related to their environment and to each other. It was also what might be described in contemporary terms as *person-centred*: the therapeutic desire was to restore the unique balance of humours that made up *this particular* healthy human being. It's the same fundamental impulse that underpins the other great humoral systems of health: the three Dhosas of Ayurveda and the Yin and Yang of traditional Chinese medicine. Contemporary integrated or complementary treatments share the same understanding: the starting-point is always the whole of a person's being and the way in which she is interacting with the myriad forces and factors that shape her life.

As the twentieth century unfolded, this holistic vision was being steadily lost by medical researchers and practitioners as they focused in on ever more particular and separate diseases. The direction of travel towards the identification of specific diseases which require specific treatments was now well established and has shown no signs of changing ever since. The benefits that this approach has brought are, of course, overwhelming. Countless millions have been rescued from the unchecked depredations of cholera, polio, diphtheria, malaria, tuberculosis, cancer and many other diseases. And yet, when applied to the tight knot of mental, emotional, physical, existential and spiritual suffering for which *depression* is shorthand, this same relentless drive to hunt down and name ever more pathologies has had a strange, and some would say, impoverishing effect.

In the course of the 1950s medical and pharmaceutical researchers stumbled by accident on the apparent mood-lifting properties of certain drugs. They had been looking at ways to treat tuberculosis and other conditions, but were struck by the renewed vigour that some of their patients seemed to display. This represented, among other things, a significant commercial opportunity for the fast-growing pharmaceutical companies. A whole new mode of treatment could now be created. As we already know, a vital part of any creation process is *naming*. Sure enough, a new name was coined: *antidepressants*. Up to this point the cluster of symptoms including insomnia, loss of appetite, absence of libido, low energy and restlessness would have been met with an ad hoc mixture of responses: medication such as sedatives and tranquillizers (which were beginning to be known as addictive) and 'nerve tonics' or – if you had money and lived in certain parts of the developed world – psychoanalysis. But now there was the intoxicating possibility of creating the longed-for *magic bullet* that would precisely eliminate exactly what we want to get rid of – and cause no harm on the way.

A bullet, magic or otherwise, requires a target. It is from the late 1950s onwards that *depression* increasingly appears as a diagnosis and as a cultural fact, accompanied ever more closely by what gave rise to it, the antidepressant. By the time the second great wave of chemical anti-depression came in the late 1980s, the idea of this disease and this particular way of treating it had become completely naturalized. This was simply the way things were. The world was on the verge of forgetting a time when depression wasn't a pandemic, with Prozac as its unquestioned cure. So it's worth paying attention to the many historians of modern medicine, and psychiatry in particular, who have claimed that this whole development – still unfolding today – has been led by the pills and those who sell them. Ever more sophisticated and targeted medication means ever more specific diagnostic categories in order to justify their production, further research and further marketing. There's a circular, self-justifying neatness in the cycle of development, which has led to the current situation where 40 million US citizens are now taking antidepressants, alongside ever-increasing numbers being prescribed specific drugs targeted at other 'new' conditions such as Obsessive Compulsive Disorder, Attention Deficit Disorder and Social Phobia. This swift, almost unnoticed, triumph of the disease model of depression and its always-available pharmaceutical solution has led one of the historians of the phenomenon to sum up our current situation in stark terms: 'In many respects the discovery of antidepressants has been the invention of and marketing of depression.' And another, even more pithily: 'Depression, in other words, was created as much as it was discovered.'

Which is not to say that before the 1950s there was no suffering of the kind that *depression* tries to describe. Ask Dr Johnson, Hamlet, the Fisher King, Job and Arjuna. It was simply understood (and undergone) in different ways and given different names, when it was called anything at all. Nor is it necessarily the case that the diagnosis of depression is so widespread simply because this is a much more depressing, fragmenting and fear-inducing world than it ever has been before. (Though the images of violence and heartlessness relentlessly delivered and addictively consumed from ever more intimate and impersonal screens might make us believe so. But there are other voices who maintain that this is the very *best* of times to be alive, citing global advances in health, wealth, inequality, the environment, peace and democracy. So, should we feel happier? How do we know? How can we tell?)

Nor is it simply the case that doctors and other health professionals are crudely wedded to the disease model and its implications. Things have moved on since the heady days when Imipramine and then Amitriptyline and then Prozac were the unquestioned kings. A General Practitioner in the UK will be aware of the psycho-bio-social model of depression when he or she is sitting for a few minutes with someone whose life seems to have drained out of them. He will know that there is a story to be heard and many factors to take into account: work, relationships, physical health, life-traumas ... She might even have a feeling that it would be good for this person to take more exercise, change their diet, take up a new activity, meet people ... Or simply be *listened to* for a long time – as long as it takes to get to the heart of the matter. But the GP only has a few minutes. The waiting room is full. The prescription pad is to hand and the supply of pills provided by the still-growing pharmaceutical companies is seemingly infinite ...

The invention and marketing of depression has tended to stifle a curiosity about the meaning and the quality of *this person's* particular suffering. Or, to stick with the language that we currently have, a curiosity about *this unique depression*, rather than depression, the impersonal disease-entity that can strike anyone at any time and can best be *defeated* by being diagnosed. The very existence of the diagnosis can act as a subliminal distraction or barrier. 'I'm having difficulty sleeping, I feel numb, I'm reluctant to go out of the house, I keep feeling terrified for no reason, I have awful thoughts about ending it all,' I say to my friend or to my doctor. 'It sounds as though you're depressed,' comes the response. Have I been helped? I'm not sure. It feels as though the attention has subtly but profoundly shifted to something other than me, called *depression*, and to my brain chemistry, rather than the (possibly mysterious) reasons why I can't sleep, feel numb, don't want to leave the house etc.

For some people, at some times, it is an enormous relief to be awarded the diagnosis of depression. If the grinding agony of the suffering has been suppressed and denied (by yourself or others), there can be a kind of liberation that comes with this recognition of the fearful experience you are going through. And there can be a double lift in the reassurance that there is medication that will help. If that does indeed work for you or for those you love, there is real cause for celebration. For myself and for many others, I know that the free-floating presence of the idea, or the diagnosis, of *depression* is like a huge black monolith which, if clung to, can obliterate an infinity of smaller, less predictable, more detailed, human-sized responses. I've often wondered what a conversation or consultation about depression would be like if we weren't allowed to use (or even think) the word *depression*. We would need to pay careful attention to the words and feelings and gestures and silences of each other. We would need to be curious and patient, to be wary of making assumptions; we would need to suspend all of our preconceptions and to listen. We would need to take our time.

In a wide-ranging essay entitled 'The Cultural Construction of Western Depression', Sushrut Jadhav, a psychiatrist and medical anthropologist, discusses the problematic meeting (or non-meeting) between the disease-entity called depression, as constructed in the West, and actual human beings who have grown up and experienced their emotional pain and confusion in a culture (India) where talk of depression really is a foreign language. The Western disease model thoroughly informs the training and the procedures of the Indian doctors. They sit with their patients, whose lives have been shaped and nurtured and sometimes broken in the villages and cities and vast expanses of India. The patients have their own Hindi words to describe what is happening to them, phrases such as: *naara mein dard*; *meetha dard*; *sar mein garmi*; *tidik*; *badan mein dard*; *dil mein udasi* ... The doctors strain to see through these local idioms to identify the universal criteria that will lead them to the diagnosis of depression or another psychiatric condition, and so to the appropriate prescription. But the very words that they are translating to themselves internally are the clues and signals that cry out for their compassionate attention: *pain in the nerves ... sweet pain ... heat in the head ... twitch ... pain in the body ... sorrow in the heart ...*

These words – the language of the people and the language of their bodies – are the all-important glimpses of what lies beneath their dulled and deadened exterior. They are like catching momentary sight of the crab's white body, vulnerable and unhoused, cringing with a remembered or anticipated pain, waiting in hopeless abandonment. Yes, we could translate these people as *depressed*. But there are more accurate and honouring words that we can use, if we can recognize them (and ourselves) as – for the moment – burdened, exhausted, fearful, broken and grieving a terrible loss.

MEDITATION: I WILL GIVE YOU REST

Jesus was a meditator. The Gospels are full of accounts of his withdrawal to lonely places to pray in silence. It is certainly meditation that he is speaking of when he gives his central teaching on prayer. He tells us to go into our 'private room' and to shut the door. Once there, we are advised not to 'heap up empty phrases'. More words, more noise, more display and more mental activity will achieve nothing at all. The 'private room' might well be the physical location that we have chosen as our regular meditation space. More significantly, it stands for the interior place within – and shared by – each of us. Beyond the incessant loops of mental commentary, judgement, anxiety and planning lies the place of simplicity and silence. It is where we come from and where we go to. A home that we rarely visit – and yet one that is constantly available to us. Like all the wisdom teachers, Jesus tells us that the less we do and the less that we desperately try to BE someone, the closer we come to this kingdom, this state of being, where there is no longer any need to struggle to protect ourselves and to survive.

It's the way of subtraction, where less is not just more, but *everything*. The same note is sounded in almost every teaching that Jesus gives. He tells his listeners that unless they become 'like children' they will never enter this kingdom, which is already there, always has been and always will be, within them and between them, waiting. He points to the lilies in the fields and to the birds of the air as role-models for how to truly live, free from the increasing complexities that we spin out of every effort-filled moment and day and year. He tells a rich young man to sell all his possessions and give to the poor. The young man can't conceive of such a thing and goes away sorrowfully. Jesus explains that unless we are prepared to identify with what the world considers as small and meaningless, then we might as well be trying to put a camel through the eye of a needle. Just too big and too much baggage to get into the kingdom.

We're not able to reverse time and actually become children again. We are – for the moment – human beings, not birds or flowers. It is probably not quite practical for us to instantly sell all our material possessions. But the teaching is clear, and speaks to us at every moment of our lives. Be prepared, Jesus says, to give up everything, to be *what looks like* less. He sums up his teaching on prayer by completing the process of subtraction. Actually, there is only *one* thing necessary, he says. Set your mind on the kingdom 'before everything else, and all the rest will come to you as well'.

What we're really being invited to give up is not our car, our house, our laptop and our multiple hand-held devices (although it would be healthier to have a much lighter grip on all of those things). The possessions that we are really fiercely attached to are much less tangible: our ideas about who we are, beliefs deeply hidden even – *especially* – from ourselves, the self-sustaining narratives that we run for reassurance over and over again.

When we're depressed it probably feels like we have already had everything taken away from us. Often it can seem as though the world has shrunk down to two overwhelming preoccupations, both of which are proving impossible to manage. First there is the burden of loss and pain that you are carrying through every moment of the day and night. You may not call it that yet, but that, in plain terms, is what it is. Something has been mislaid – let's call it your life – and strangely this painful absence has turned into the constant presence of a dead weight from which you feel unable to escape. The second thing that is going on is your effort to hide all of this from yourself and from others. Here is where all the energy leaks away. The struggle to keep it all together, to be the 'self' that you and others expect you to be, is the truly exhausting self-imposed task. This is the Buddhist second arrow of suffering, striking deeper and deeper. Suffering about suffering.

The greatest gift a human being in distress can receive is the presence of someone to whom they can tell their pain. A family member, a lover, a compassionate stranger, a therapist – at the moment of attentive listening each of them is a true friend. Whether such a person is present in our lives or not, when we sit to meditate we enter into the way of friendship. In meditation we no longer have to hide our sense of nothingness and smallness. It is known, it is a given and it is accepted. The relief can be overwhelming and deeply healing. If we can speak of a gift that depression offers, it is the way that it brings our unprotected vulnerability so close to the surface. In meditation we can for a blessed moment stop pretending that we have nothing in common with the unhoused crab caught between places of safety. We will all have much work to do, and much grace to receive, outside of our times of meditation, finding places to shelter and people to take refuge with. But unless we are able to acknowledge our fundamental nakedness, without denying it and without scuttling away, we will not find the entrance to our kingdom. Where is that kingdom? Exactly here, and exactly now, as we breathe in and out in stillness, simplicity and silence.

Remember to sit comfortably with your back straight. Allow yourself to be aware of how your body is feeling, where there is any pain, any tightness or clenching, any areas of warmth or coldness. Acknowledge all of that and simply let it be. Notice your mental activity. What is the tempo of your mind at this moment? Are your thoughts sluggish and incomplete? Are they racing, moving swiftly from one temporary perch to another? Let it all begin to settle as you lay thoughts and sensations aside, bringing your attention gently to one single point, allowing everything else to fall away, to be subtracted. Because the kingdom is not a place or a possession, choose to place your attention on your breath, that vital 'nothing' that we keep being given and that we keep giving away. And, if you choose to, let the breath gently carry that other vital 'nothing', the mantra, from the beginning of the meditation to the end, as you set your mind on the kingdom. Not a place or a possession, nor an achievement or a reward, but a friendship. *Maranatha ... Maranatha ... Maranatha ...*

Before meditation:

Come to me, all who are weary and burdened, and I will give you rest. Take my yoke upon you and learn from me, for I am gentle and humble in heart, and you will find rest for your souls. For my yoke is easy and my burden is light.

Matthew 11.28–30

Meditate for 20 minutes
(or for however long you have discovered your
practice to be)

After meditation:

*He who binds to himself a joy
Does the wingèd life destroy;
But he who kisses the joy as it flies
Lives in eternity's sunrise.*

William Blake

LOSS, GRIEF, MOURNING AND BIRDWINGS

A word of encouragement about your meditation practice. You may be tempted to beat yourself up about it, to find more reasons for dejection and despair: *I didn't get anywhere near the kingdom, whatever that is. I can't 'lay aside' my thoughts. There was nothing gentle about it – and I still don't know what friendship is. Stillness, simplicity and silence? It just confirmed to me that I'm restless, complicated and noisy. Yet another thing hasn't worked for me. I've failed again …*

Responses like this, or variations of them, often happen when people begin to meditate, and frequently recur as the practice grows, is abandoned and then taken up again. The first thing you experience, probably every time that you sit down to meditate, is just how widely scattered or even chaotic your thoughts and the energies of your body have become. But even this very awareness is a seemingly small, but vitally important triumph. To become conscious of the random and disordered nature of your experience, and then to set about witnessing and tolerating it, means that you are already on the path of transformation. Rather than being unconsciously lost, you have now *found* that you are lost. Unknown unknowns have at least turned into known unknowns. This is now a different world, the possibility of a new creation.

Further encouragement: John Main, the great teacher of meditation within the Christian contemplative tradition said, half-jokingly, that the first 20 years of your practice will be the most difficult. (But don't forget that it was also John Main who tells us, with joyful seriousness, that our meditation will take as long as it takes to realize that it takes no time at all.) It all becomes much simpler if we can remember what Tibetan Buddhist teachers tell their students: that meditation is just the awareness of whatever occurs.

We find this simple practice so difficult because our restlessness is of such intensity and – unless acknowledged and befriended – so all-consuming. This constant mental and emotional searching (so constant that most of the time we don't even notice it) is our doomed attempt to secure our safety, to make sure that we remain intact. We are unconsciously driven by the nagging sense that something will be missing if, for a moment, we interrupt the flow of thoughts, fantasies and plans that keep us in existence. Loss – of any kind – is our greatest fear. Until we admit that fact to ourselves and bring the monster blinking out into the light, it will also be the fear that drives everything we do. At some level, justifiably based on experiences that keep on happening from the moment we are born, we all know the deep truth of the famous and scandalous Zen saying that life is like stepping onto a boat which is about to sail out to sea and sink.

Conspiring to keep that a secret is what brings us to slow and steady disaster. It makes our searching and our loss-avoidance compulsive and never-ending. Uncovering the secret in each other's company, with as open a heart as possible, changes everything. That, at least, is what I have learned at times of meditation – times that could also have easily been described as distracted, restless, failed. Often I was lucky enough to be meditating with others. Sometimes, I'm sure, we all gave up. But the gift of practising together helped us to never *give up*.

LOSS AND WOUNDING

As the noise in my dying ear relentlessly increased, the distorted sounds of the city grew more shocking and invasive. Every day I felt less qualified to join in with life as lived by other people. I did what depressed people do – I started to avoid social contact and other human beings in general. My attendance at the weekly meditation group also became more intermittent. One day, when I had forced myself to go back there, a sympathetic retired doctor listened compassionately to my faltering reports of how I was doing. 'Hearing,' she said, 'it's such a fundamental part of our relationship with the world, isn't it? And our sense of self. Even more so than sight somehow. It's no wonder that you're experiencing a reactive depression.'

Her kind words helped, sort of. Though they couldn't quite penetrate the fog that surrounded my whole being. By the time they reached me they had been slowed down by the weather-shroud in which I was still hidden; they fell against me in a drizzle of tumbling letters. What definitely got through was that phrase 'reactive depression'. I had somehow forgotten that one of the classic distinctions made by doctors is that between a 'reactive' depression and one that is 'endogenous'. In other words, a mood disorder for which there is a clear *external* reason (reactive), and one where the 'stressor' is *internal* (endogenous). In the diagnostic literature these internal factors are further identified as being *cognitive* or *biological*. (The external ones, for what it's worth, are classified as *environmental* and *social*.) Hearing the phrase again now, I was reminded that I had long ago realized that it meant very little to me. Living my life, and being alongside others living theirs, had taught me that, actually, *all depression is reactive*. To know this we just need to slow down, patiently allow our gaze to widen and learn to see in the dark.

***

Each life is an unlikely miracle. As unlikely, says the Buddha, as a blind turtle which surfaces from an infinite ocean only once in a hundred years, rising to put its head through a gold ring that shifts and floats forever on the water. That is the heart-expanding miracle of your life. *And* your life is also a series of losses. (There is surely a boat somewhere near that gold-crowned turtle, steadily sinking.) From the moment we are born (and perhaps even before) we are responding – reacting – to loss of one kind or another.

Birth is a kind of exile – we lose our first home and, with it, an experience of profound unity and safety. (Though there are many whose pre-birth experiences will have had very little of security or welcome about them.) As we grow, we will encounter, at some level, the loss of the exclusive attention of the one who holds us and feeds us and protects us. *There are other people in the world!* Our first taste of the loss of status and power. And so we continue to grow into a life in which we secretly know that any and all of our gains could also be our losses. My lover, my house, my reputation, my job, my friend, my safety, my health, my control over my body and my life ... they could disappear at any time. And, in fact, they will. So I hold on to them tightly, because without them I believe that I will cease to exist.

The cataclysm of my hearing loss wasn't the first time that I had experienced a depression. Thirty-five years before that I had felt, over a period of months, something that I had never felt before. A swiftly creeping sensation that seemed to set in over a few days. My body was draining of life, with flesh and blood turning into metal and stone. Everything tasted and smelt and felt like cardboard. And concealed somewhere in this suddenly infinite desert were a couple of nuclear bombs. Eventually I realized that they were in me. I didn't know that it was possible to be so terrified and so inert at the same time. All of this had seemingly been triggered because an ex-girlfriend, with whom I was still on good terms, had started a romantic relationship with another friend of mine. I didn't know it until it happened, but this was the *exact* combination that would set off a deeply toxic reaction in me. Within days I felt mute, leaden and worthless.

What had I lost that had reduced me so quickly to this state? Not simply those two friendships; it turned out that there was a lot more at stake. Luckily I found someone who was able to help me defuse those bombs – or rather, detonate them in a controlled explosion in a therapy room in West London. Painfully, crawling over what felt like every inch of this new desert, I began to know that what I had lost in this recent drama was a particular image of myself. Featuring me as someone special and unique (which I am, as we all are, but not in the way that I thought). And as I sat or crawled or lay down and listened over and over again to the explosions going off in my body, I began to know that these were echoes of much, much earlier losses. In my case: the loss of permission to be other than perfect and perfectly in control; the prohibition of anger; the denial of my right to be anything other than happy. Together these added up to the most catastrophic loss of all, the one that very few of us escape from: the loss of the right – even the ability – to be fully *me*, to be fully *you*.

In his brilliant book *The New Black: Mourning, Melancholia and Depression*, psychoanalyst Darian Leader gets to the heart of what is happening every time we experience a loss – at any age – which disastrously changes our sense of being a person of any value. In each instance, he says, 'an ideal image of ourselves as lovable is punctured'. This is what we are always reacting to, from the moment that we become conscious: this threatened assault on, or even annihilation of, the self. If depression results, it only looks 'endogenous' because we lack the vision to see the infinity of factors impacting on every human life at every moment. Just in the way that we don't know *which* flap of *which* butterfly's wing will cause a distant hurricane several weeks later on, much of the internal wounding from our life-losses takes place beyond the reach of our sight. The tragedy is that most of it is happening in front of our very eyes.

GRIEF AND MOURNING

At the bottom of the heart of every human being, from earliest infancy until the tomb, there is something that goes on indomitably expecting, in the teeth of all experience of crimes committed, suffered, and witnessed, that good and not evil will be done to him. It is this above all that is sacred in every human being.

This extraordinary affirmation is made by Simone Weil, the Jewish Christian philosopher and contemplative, in her essay 'Human Personality', published in 1943. Every time I read these words I have a strong image of the baby that each of us once was and – in our hidden places – still is. (And now I catch, too, another glimpse of that crab, naked and expectant in Patagonian waters, waiting for the gift of its next home.) Simone Weil's words speak of the most fundamental orientation of our nature. Our default setting – one that is never quite fully eradicated – is the innocent expectation that we will be met, cared for, loved. At whatever stage in our life we encounter the disappointment of this expectation, we will have an experience of wounding, loss and grief. The way we are able to deal with this grief lies at the very heart of how we will grow as human beings.

One of the most common and most visible responses to loss is anger and blame. Whatever or whoever makes us feel in pain and diminished is the target of our anger – sometimes rage. Often the same impulse is turned against ourselves. We lose something that we treasure – usually the positive regard of another – and we decide at some deep level that it must be our fault. That 'ideal image of ourselves as lovable' has been punctured one more time. It is one of the scandals of being human that it is so often the one who suffers the loss brought about by humiliation, abandonment, abuse or neglect who ends up feeling worthless and full of the shame that properly belongs to someone else.

Many of us get stuck in blame or anger, humiliation or guilt for the rest of our lives. But if we are able in some way to replay and slow down our responses to our wounding and our losses, we will be able to see that – even before the reactive anger and defensiveness that inevitably follows the shock of pain – something else is present: grief. This grief is the sadness implied by Simone Weil's world-changing insight. That somewhere in our being we have always expected, and always will expect, to be met with the opposite of loss – which is love. But instead, we keep on meeting the inevitable disappointments and deficits of life; we question our own lovability, and so we grieve, ever more secretly, ever more alone.

In *The New Black*, Darian Leader makes a vital distinction. 'Mourning,' he says, 'is different from grief. Grief is our reaction to a loss, but mourning is how we process this grief.' If, as individuals or as a culture, we find that ways of mourning are not available to us, or if we never even have a thought about mourning, then there is a danger that our grief will be stillborn. It may just be that what we call depression grows – and stays – primarily because we don't know what to do with our grief. No one has ever given us the opportunity to mourn. Instead of being taken forward by the movement that is the process of mourning, we will recoil from our grief as just too painful to bear. We will take shelter in the bunkers of anger, blame, denial and distraction that will inexorably turn – if we spend too long there – into anxiety and depression. What is being played out are the doomed twin strategies of denial on the one hand, and complete identification on the other. We can pretend that our grief doesn't exist and try to live in the smoke-screen of displacement activities, addiction or driven over-achievement. Or we can end up forging an identity out of our pain, somehow falling for the powerful illusion that we are nothing other than the sum of all our woundings. Either way, you eventually find that your pain is running your life, and you – if you have any energy left – are running on the spot.

So, what is mourning? The word probably conjures up images of mirrors turned to the wall, Victorian figures dressed in black, shutters closed, curtains drawn. Indeed, the end of the nineteenth century *was* the last time that our culture – certainly British culture – had a shared public language and iconography of mourning. Some historians maintain that the First World War brought all that to an end. There were just too many deaths; mourning became meaningless – the extent of the carnage somehow rendered us collectively mute and paralysed. Did we ever recover from that? Some would point to high-profile times of 'collective outpourings of grief' such as those provoked by Princess Diana's death and other celebrity funerals. But increasingly these become – like everything else in the public realm – part of the swiftly vanishing newsfeed, the world of arising, disappearing and quickly forgotten images. Mourning is now as likely as anything else to be a shared and liked meme rather than a rite of passage through which a community allows its members to grieve and grow.

Yet for those who are bereaved, there is still an acknowledged language of sorts, even though it has been greatly privatized. From a small withered bouquet on a lamp-post, to the stern hearses that hold up the traffic on the way to the cemetery, we still recognize the traces of mourning. And yet, because it has become much less of a collective undertaking, it has somehow also become curtailed. There is an expectation that mourning will be over and done with after a set period – a certain number of months or perhaps, at its most generous, a year or two. If the grieving and mourning process is so impoverished when there is certifiable evidence of an actual death, how are we to deal with all the other wounding losses of our lives? The series of hasty burials that our bodies are full of? The deaths that we die before we die?

For wounding, loss and grief to become mourning – an active process that helps us to live as fully as possible with our pain – one thing is necessary: connection to others. Attentive listening is what draws us from the dumb prison that deeply buried grief can become. The listening might start with the simplest but most important of questions. The Fisher King is only released from his frozen death-in-life when the knight Parzifal, constantly searching for the Holy Grail, asks him the question that changes everything: *What ails thee, friend?* Instantly spring returns to the land, the pond thaws and the wounded king is healed. He is able to tell Parzifal that the Holy Grail is just over the hill. Last time he passed this way, 30 years before, the much younger Parzifal had only asked the direct question: *Where is the Holy Grail?* and had been met with silence. Being interested in the other, asking the question, and being truly ready to hear the response, is what brings about transformation. Not always as instantaneously as in the story of the stricken king, yet the myth still speaks its powerful truth to us. This deep understanding of fellowship, this empathy, *is itself* the Holy Grail.

Where can we expect to find this attentive listening which will ask us in many different ways: *what ails thee?* At its best, this is the generous invitation that is extended by practitioners of psychotherapy and counselling and anyone else who is prepared to take an open-hearted interest in another. *Tell me your story, if you have words to tell it. If they're not there, let's find them together, or discover what gestures or sounds or movement or silences speak most truthfully from the places where you have buried your pain.* If we are very lucky there may be others in our lives – friends or compassionate strangers – who are able to be alongside us in a similar way. If we have been told – or have told ourselves – that we are depressed, and that somehow that is an end of it, the invaluable work that they help us to do is to begin to give other names to this thing called depression: truer names like *loss, wounding, grief, mourning*, and – most importantly of all – they can help us to name it as *an opportunity*: to learn, to heal and to flourish.

St Augustine seemed to experience a profound knowing of the way in which the damage that we endure can be the beginning of something, and not just the finality that we so often take it to be: 'In my deepest wound I saw your glory, and it dazzled me.'

BIRDWINGS

From our birth, what emerges out of the losses, griefs and restorations that we successively undergo is a more or less workable 'self'. We then present this to the world, and back to ourselves, to confirm our continuing existence. It's a kind of shelter that we construct – without even thinking about it – out of the chapter of accidents which is our unfolding life. A life that sometimes folds back in on itself, and when growth seems stalled for a while. 'Self' has collapsed again, only to recover once more into a new formation, one that may now be more closed, or more open, depending on how far we've been able truly to mourn what we've lost. This ongoing self-improvisation isn't really something that we consciously *do* for ourselves. All of the countless forces that surround us shape the shell that grows and that turns into what we – and everybody else – naturally take to be *my self*.

This *conditioned self* (to give it one of its names) is always going to bear some marks of something that seems like depression. As the baby, the child, the young person gets older, she grows through a series of compromises and negotiations in response to losses and griefs, both large and small. (Although my body-memory tells me that all griefs seem large when *you* are small.) The organism is adjusting to the gap between what it expects and what it encounters. You could say that it is becoming more realistic, and so, more real. Deep-seated fantasies of omnipotence and total security are painfully relinquished as the embattled, would-be tyrant (the growing child) is allowed to mourn its way into becoming a person capable of recognizing and valuing the experience of others, of whom she is one. The positive and healing aspects of the process are reflected in the psychoanalytic language for a child's development, which sees him moving (naturally and healthily) from the *paranoid-schizoid* position (fearful, defended, no secure sense of self) to the *mature depressive* position (capable of mutuality, not dominated by anxiety, fear or aggression). Some element of depression – renamed as loss, grief and mourning – is clearly a universal and necessary experience, and one that can lead to resilience and growth.

Some are more wounded – and more catastrophically wounded – than others. For many, the shell is formed and fixed at an early age. The healthy progression of wounding, loss, grief and mourning is arrested before it really gets going. Our conditioned self might have grown such a thick skin that it will tend to cut us off from the contact with others that we secretly crave. The reality of our pain is just too deeply buried. Or our defences never even get a chance to form and we feel hardly covered at all – the wound and the fear always lying painfully close to the surface. (Which is why the thick skin grows in the first place. How close the 'hiddenness' of depression and the 'exposure' of anxiety really are.) Either way, our protective layer will be prone to cracking open (like a crab shell) at significant moments.

This breaking can be an unexpected gift. Without it, how will we be able to move on to the next formation of the shell, our next home? 'Getting stuck' is really just a necessary breaking that needs to happen *right now*, but which we desperately and steadfastly ignore. Perhaps because we believe that no one is prepared to help us move house. Perhaps because of the terror of the imagined pain that moving will bring. And anyway, there is no new home waiting – not for *me*. Some people get stuck for years, some for a whole life. It's an obvious scandal to suggest that depression and anxiety can bring us gifts and opportunities. Nobody (or almost nobody) will ever choose to experience that amount of distress. And it's just plain wrong and heartless to ever suggest to someone that 'suffering is good for you'. And yet what these experiences can clumsily offer, but with infinite grace, is the disruption of our comfortable – sometimes extremely *un*comfortable – assumptions about where our home lies or whether we have one at all.

The agony turns into gift if it helps us to an awareness that this conditioned self, this shelter that I have helped to build around me and in me, is not my ultimate home. It is as real as anything else in this world, but it is also provisional – like *everything* else in the world. The shock and the insult of anxiety and depression can be a teaching about where we truly live. We cannot make a permanent home in either our wounds or the shelters we construct to stop the wounding from ever happening again. We wanted to live in the grand distant palaces we were promised, but setting out for them we got hurt, so now we've taken to our bunkers …

What we are always on the point of learning – even at our most numbed and terrified, perhaps *especially* at these times – is that none of these places is our true home. Our true home is the very movement that we are too frightened – or that we believe ourselves too friendless – to make. It is a simple movement into the gaps, the welcoming space that exists between all these temporary locations. It is a movement of opening and closing, receiving and releasing, losing and mourning, only to be surprised by something unexpected and new. This is the only real life there is – sitting, befriended, among the beautiful wreckage of everything that we've ever built.

> Your grief for what you've lost lifts a mirror
> up to where you are bravely working.
> Expecting the worst, you look, and instead,
> here's the joyful face you've been wanting to see.
> Your hand opens and closes and opens and closes.

If it were always a fist or always stretched open,
you would be paralysed.
Your deepest presence is in every small contracting and
expanding,
the two as beautifully balanced and coordinated
as birdwings.

Rumi

MEDITATION – 'A MOMENT IN EACH DAY'

Sometimes we spend every second of every day either overwhelmed by dejection and despair or doing everything we can to hold them at arm's length. This is the most tiring work in the world, and your arms never get any longer. If we choose to set aside time each day for meditation, we are creating a space in which we are able to profoundly change the nature of the struggle. There *is* another way.

During the time of meditation we are consciously deciding not to identify with the feelings and sensations that seem so threatening and toxic to our lives. Nor are we pushing them away and denying their existence. We simply sit with them and allow them to be there, while changing our relationship to them forever by placing our attention *elsewhere*: on the rising and falling of the mantra, our breath, or the two of them mingled together. When we do this we are inviting a moment into each day of our lives in which the forces of relentless conditioning – the stored history of our minds and our bodies – can be put into complete suspension. It's the slipping into neutral of *karma*; the relief that comes when the punishing march of cause-and-effect is allowed at last to break step. William Blake describes it beautifully when he talks of the 'Moment in each Day that Satan cannot find'.

When we remember that the root meaning of *satan* in Hebrew is *accuser, enemy* or *obstacle* then we start to know just what our times of meditation can be. They begin to act as *clearings* in our day. Perhaps, at first, just moments, during which self-punishment, resentment, weariness and stuckness are not completely in control. But as you persist in meditation, these tentative moments become more confident of their own existence, increasingly able to connect with each other. Their unfamiliar emptiness might even begin to feel like a strange new home, yet one that somehow, from somewhere, you have always known. This is no miracle cure, nor a magic bullet, but it *is* the ground of transformation. Blake spells it out in his next few lines:

There is a Moment in each Day that Satan cannot find
Nor can his Watch Fiends find it, but the Industrious find
This Moment & it multiply, & when it once is found
It Renovates every Moment of the Day if rightly placed ...

If we are exhausted by depression, guilt, self-accusation and hopelessness, what chance do we have of becoming *Industrious*? The question is inevitable and arises naturally from the place of grinding labour that existence becomes when all vitality seems lost. And yet I love the idea of meditators as *the Industrious*. Meditation has been described as the work of attention and as the work of love. Simone Weil reminds us constantly that these two are inseparable. Perhaps our simple act of sitting and consciously placing our attention elsewhere is the discovery of a work that refreshes. It can certainly be the beginning of the end of a very different kind of work – the crushing slavery of constantly trying to overcome or avoid being overcome by the obstacles and accusers that seem to surround us and inhabit us. The *renovation* that Blake talks of then begins to feel like resurrection. And *rightly placed* doesn't mean meditating at an exact time of day, or in a particularly sacred place (they all are), or even doing it with the right people, or the right amount of ceremony. And it definitely doesn't mean *getting it right*. *Rightly placed* simply means being placed among the banal and intimate moments of *your* life, in the face of whatever suffering there might be, here and now.

Antidepressants may have a role to play in any experience of recovery. Used crudely, though, they can simply be a way of saying *No* to depression and everything that it might be wanting to say – all the other names for which it is acting as a pseudonym. The daily practice of meditation is a way of saying *Yes* to whatever is present, welcoming even depression and the pain that it is masking or compensating for. It will probably be a grudging and a cautious welcome to start with. It may bring guests – anger, hurt, panic, hopelessness, fear, to name a few who are often on the list – that you find you need the help of others to deal with. Or it may prove to be a place where you can hang out with these new arrivals who you've met in your counsellor's consulting room or wherever else you've been able to find sanctuary and companionship. Either way, it becomes a process of befriending. And somewhere in the process of befriending there is always a *Yes* to be found.

In a *Yes* there is always vulnerability. In our meditation practice we are creating a new emptiness which can, paradoxically, become a container for our work of mourning. At the heart of this mourning is the real work of the really *Industrious*: our saying of *Yes* to what we think will kill us, or already has done. Our *Yes* is not to victimhood. It is the beginning of knowing who we are and of acknowledging that the places we took to be our homes can all too easily become our prisons if we cling on to them too tightly. A Buddhist prizes the three jewels – the Buddha, the Dharma and the Sangha (the Awakened One, his teaching and the community of those who try to live it) as the place where she *takes refuge*. It's a way of living with the full knowledge of our radically homeless state. In meditating together (you're always meditating *together* even if you are practising in a room by yourself) we are not building a refuge of total individual security; we are inviting our wounds and our continuing vulnerability to be present, and, as our practice continues, to shed their names and their power over us, in the shelter of our shared silence.

- Sit comfortably with your back straight and take a few moments to come home to your body, your mantra, your breath.
- Lay aside your thoughts by allowing your awareness to be more than just what seems to be in your head. Feel the presence of the breath and the mantra in the rest of your body – in your shoulders, your chest, your belly, where you're sitting on a chair or a stool, and in your feet upon the ground. Is everything below the neck another welcoming home that you've strangely

neglected until this moment? Even with its pains, its tightness, its apparent obstacles? Can you simply begin to befriend your body, along with everything else that is present right now?

- Settle gently into this lower place, this different way of knowing, without words, without names.

Before meditation:

For here we have no abiding city ...

Hebrews 13.14

Meditate for 20 minutes

After meditation:

Not knowing when the dawn will come,
I open every door.

Emily Dickinson

NO SELF/NO SHORTCUTS

Before we can surrender ourselves we must become ourselves. No one can give up what they do not possess.

Thomas Merton

I was about to write that I clearly remember the first time I sat in formal meditation. But just as I began to recall the scene, it flashed across my memory that this was in fact the *second* time. (Maybe this is how it always is with recollections of contemplative emptiness and silence? The great insight of meditation is that we are always beginners. Which must apply backwards as well as forwards into the future. Perhaps we can wake to an infinitely regressing memory of ourselves as meditators? What about that time sitting on the wall in the playground, aged about six, gazing through the sunlight at nothing in particular? What about the time that only my body remembers, when I was curled in the boundless hush of my mother's womb, like the star child in the movie of *2001: A Space Odyssey*? Always beginning.)

The *first* time of formal meditation was during my early months at university – around 1975. One day my closest friend and I decided that we had done enough drinking and reading for the moment. What about learning to meditate? The suggestion came, I think, primarily from John. He had just changed his course of study from English to Divinity and the idea that we should get cross-legged was simply another part of his ever-widening exploration. I agreed to go along for the ride. The prospect seemed impossibly exotic and, frankly, cool. I hadn't yet been given Merton's *Zen and the Birds of Appetite* but I was open to the allure of The East. It was, after all, only seven years since The Beatles had spent time with the Maharishi in Rishikesh, firmly linking the burgeoning counter-culture with the technique of Transcendental Meditation as developed by their new teacher. (Though they themselves were somewhat behind the curve: his world tour had started in 1958.)

We rather nervously found our way to an introductory class in TM one gloomy winter's evening in the land of the Fens. My recollections of the session, of our fellow students, and of the teacher are all pretty sketchy. He may well have been bearded and wearing white, but that might just as easily be a reconstruction based on lingering images of the iconic 'giggling guru' and his characteristic presentation over many decades. What I do vividly remember is what happened as soon as the greetings and the time of instruction were over. Having taken all this teaching in, we were invited to put it into practice, to sit in silent, non-judgemental, loving awareness.

As soon as we all positioned ourselves, with varying degrees of self-consciousness, on the cushions and stools provided, a calm and reassuring silence fell. Almost immediately, the back street that the open window of the meditation room gave on to erupted into a cacophony of systematically breaking glass. A hoarse voice shouted insults into the air and celebrated incoherently each time there was another shattering of bottles against the pavement. The sound of dustbins being kicked over and banged together added to the fractured chaos that carried on floating through the window for the whole (so memory now says) of our meditation. Every time the silence seemed to have settled once more, a snarl of drunken rage would rise up and then die away again. At the end of the class, John and I said polite farewells to the teacher and then leaned against the walls outside in the darkness, crying and wheezing with laughter. We didn't go back.

The next time that I was invited to sit in calm abiding and just witness my thoughts and sensations, letting them go as soon as I became aware of them, was in a team meeting when I was working with a homeless charity near Portobello Market in West London. This was six years after the glass-smashing meditation. I was part of a paid staff-team of four who coordinated a much larger group of live-in volunteers. They lived and worked with the residents of our hostels, choosing to exist on the same meagre benefits that were available to the homeless. A regular feature of our full team meetings was the invitation for one of the volunteers to lead an information or training session for the benefit of the rest of us. The theme or topic was entirely their choice. One of the volunteers, David, had just discovered a Buddhist community and the practice of meditation that they followed. It was this practice that David offered to share with us in the hot and cramped office where we had our meeting.

I was feeling immensely pressured – on the point of being overwhelmed – by my new job. As Resettlement Worker, I had at my disposal a tiny quota of flats across a couple of boroughs, and scores of homeless people besieging me for their chance to live in one. *Where's my flat?* was the understandable greeting, every time I met any of our residents. I was also in a strangely euphoric and anxiety-provoking emotional state. I had recently fallen in love in a way that had exploded everything in my life. My head and my heart were spinning. So I was very ready to follow David's invitation to sit as comfortably as possible, to simply notice my breath and just to witness – without grasping and without pushing away – anything that arose in my field of experience – mental, emotional, physical, even spiritual. I think we meditated for about 15 minutes. It seemed to me a lifetime – *and* the twinkling of an eye. When we finished, David asked everyone how the experience had been. There were some polite remarks, some further questions about the technique, a few raised eyebrows. When it was my turn I simply said that it was wonderful, one of the most amazing experiences I'd ever had. In all honesty, I had no way of putting it into words. I felt completely ecstatic, profoundly energized, my whole being rinsingly clarified. In the idiom of the time, I suppose I was *blissed out*. All of my anxieties and worries just fell away. I had cracked it; this was the solution to everything. There were never going to be any more problems – I could always go to this place where everything was instantly solved, because *I* didn't really exist, and nor did anything else …

***

Those first two sessions of formal sitting neatly sum up the almost universal experience of what it is to take up meditation. When people start the practice they usually encounter one or both of two mental and emotional states. Famously, what you're most likely to discover is the presence of 'monkey mind'. This is the shocking realization that your thoughts are leaping from one half-dealt-with subject to another in a swift jump-cut sequence of fantasy, obsession, planning, day-dreaming, regret and boredom. You might also become aware – perhaps for the first time – that you've been riding uneasily on a roiling sea of chaotic emotions. There is anger, hurt, resentment, fear; there's an inner drunk wanting to smash bottles and bang dustbin-lids together, roaring into the dark of the night.

Or something else might happen. You find yourself blissfully cut off from all of that chaos. A kind of 'holy floating' kicks in. All is calm, all is resolved, all is smoothed out. There is no more anger, no more fear. No bottles, no drunks. The trace of a beatific smile plays on your lips. You think it may look like the one that you've seen on the face of the reclining Buddha. Serenely, you wonder about the sound of one dustbin-lid banging.

It may not happen exactly like that, but I think these are two predictable, and probably entirely inevitable, tendencies when beginning the practice of meditation. (And, as we have to keep acknowledging, we never stop beginning. And carrying on with the practice will keep us honest.) The more dangerous tendency is probably the second one. When you're hit with the full force of the monkey mind, at least you're being confronted with *what is*. Meditation, at its most fundamental, is precisely the ability to tolerate, and then to be in relationship with, what is. It is the practice of the real. But when the blissful holy floating starts, and that's where you're determined to stay, then you are really lost. At this point you have surrendered to daydreaming. And, as Simone Weil says of the daydream, the only problem with it is that it is not real.

The blissful state is very seductive. It may well be what attracts many people to meditation in the first place. Could it be that it will act as a tranquilliser, a stimulant or an antidepressant, but without any of the side-effects, or even the cost? I know that there must have been a lot of this going on for me as I kept being drawn to meditation over the years. Surely this will be a way to simplify life, to get away from the unresolved, messy and – frankly – unacceptable parts of myself? As ever, Thomas Merton had got there before me. Look again at the quote at the beginning of this chapter. *We have to become ourselves before we can surrender ourselves.* Words that should be printed on the T-shirt of every would-be meditator. Merton returns to this theme over and over again. He knew whereof he spoke: 'Let no one hope to find in contemplation an escape from conflict, from anguish or from doubt.'

Not an escape, though we *can* expect to be found by an unlooked-for ability to rest at the absolute centre of our conflict, anguish and doubt – like someone able to sleep peacefully in a boat on a storm-ravaged sea.

SCRAMBLED EGOS

Throughout his writings Merton makes it plain that what contemplation will not enable us to escape from – certainly in any simplistic sense – is ourselves. In fact, such an escape would be an utter disaster. Like all followers of all wisdom traditions, and like contemporary teachers of meditation rooted in these traditions, Merton draws our attention to the existence of two selves. Most commonly he describes these selves as, on the one hand, *an illusory person: a false self,* and on the other, the *true self* which is *hidden with Christ in God.* This is the universal language of the wisdom teacher. Ramana Maharshi distinguishes between the 'I' of the personal self and the Self which is the 'Source of all' and which speaks its truth from the depths of every heart. (The simple shift from the lower case of *self* to the upper case of *Self* is more than a world of difference.) Others talk about the *false self* using a variety of descriptions: it is a self that is *passing, small, floating, conventional* … A shorthand that is often used is the simple word *ego.*

Simple but potentially confusing. We all know what is meant if a politician, a sportsperson or the boss is described as having a *big ego.* They are full of themselves, they tend to overlook the needs and feelings of others, their behaviour is organized entirely around what is good for *them.* Alongside this everyday usage is something much more specialized and technical. Over a hundred years ago Sigmund Freud produced the most celebrated and influential model of the human psyche when he described it as being made up of the *id,* the *ego* and the *super-ego.* (Although Freud actually used words which were much less arcane and mystifying. In the original German he talked of *Es, Ich* and *Über-Ich* which simply translate as *It*, *I* and *over-I*.) The *id* represents that part of us which is instinctive and primitive; it is the home of our appetites, our sexuality, everything that we need for our survival; immediate satisfaction and self-preservation at all costs is all that matters. The *super-ego* is that supposedly 'higher' set of functions which judges, differentiates, aspires towards perfection, punishes and drives unforgivingly on. This is the home of all of the ideals and 'shoulds' which, if unrecognized, can render so many lives aridly joyless and exhausting. The psychoanalytic and psychological understanding of the *ego* is as a version of the self which emerges as the result of a negotiation between the other two, the *super-ego* and the *id*. The nature of the internal deal that's been struck – the conditions attached to the bargain – will determine whether your *ego* is going to be a vehicle which is more or less fit for the purpose of carrying and communicating your life.

Those are the fundamentals of psychoanalytic personality theory in a nutshell. When teachers of meditation talk about the *ego*, they tend to mean something different from all of the above. In our practice of meditation we are being invited to live from a consciousness which is humble and simple but which knows no limits. In allowing our ego-consciousness to fall away we are not abandoning a particular part of the self that is 'bad' and not wanted on this voyage. In meditation the *ego* that we are loosening our grip on is nothing other than *everything* that we take ourselves to be: my thoughts, my beliefs, my feelings, my depression, my plans, my regrets, my history – in short, my identity.

It's a mistake, though, to think of this as the need to *get rid of* or to *destroy* or even to *transform* the ego. It's enough just to start to see the ego for what it is. It is neither good nor bad, desirable or undesirable, true or false; *it simply has its limits*. (Which is why it has always seemed to me often more accurate and helpful to talk of the *limited self* rather than the ego.) As long as we continue to confuse the partial truth of our limited consciousness with the full truth of that which has no limits, we will be locked in unreality, the very opposite of being awake. We will be seeing in a glass darkly and not even be aware of it. It is as absurd, and as unreal, as a drop of water denying that it is also the ocean. Or the candle flame insisting that it has nothing to do with the conflagrations of the forests, the volcanoes and the stars. The root identity – the unlimited Self – of the drop is water; the unlimited Self of the flame is fire.

This is how we need to understand the central teachings of both Jesus and the Buddha about the nature of the self. Both Matthew and Luke report Jesus saying some words which might stand as the essential instruction before each of our times of meditation for the rest of our lives. If misunderstood and heard *only* as an injunction to follow a particular code of moral behaviour, they could lead to a joyless life of self-punishment and self-denial. But if they are heard as the words of a teacher of consciousness about how to live *and* pray, then they release us from the stifling, self-imposed limits that perpetuate our suffering and keep us unreal.

If anyone wishes to be a follower of mine, he must leave self behind; he must take up his cross and come with me. Whoever cares for his own safety is lost; but if a man will let himself be lost for my sake, he will find his true self.

This is what we are doing – men and women – when we sit down to meditate. We agree to lose ourselves on purpose. Softening the walls of our small, overdefended self; letting it at last become permeable; allowing our consciousness, with its temporarily limited capacity to love and to be loved, to unite with the limitless.

Freedom from the constraints of the self also lies at the heart of the Buddha's teaching. Our craving for the illusory safety of a fixed identity (a separate self) is at the root of all our misery and dissatisfaction. The Buddha's realization of *anatta*, or no-self, is the culmination of his deep meditation at the foot of the bodhi tree. He sees the conditioned self for what it is: a provisional cluster of features, an improvised bundle. It feels real enough, but in the end, it's not. *The Dhammapada* records his lyrical words of victory as the self falls away into the freedom of emptiness. They might stand as the essential epilogue after each of our times of meditation for the rest of our lives. The small self need never again hold us prisoner:

O housebuilder, now you are seen!
You will not build the house again:
all your rafters have been broken,
and the ridgepole has been destroyed.

APPEARING HOLY; BEING SANE

The Tibetan Buddhist teacher Chögyam Trungpa once said that it is easier to appear holy than to be sane. He knew how far the reach of the ego wants to extend. The ego, or limited self, is that part of us which wants to insist that it is all of us. It will fight to the death to maintain this status quo. It sometimes seems that there is no end to its defensive strategies. Everything can become a project of the ego and its grandiose ambitions. Thomas Merton was well aware of this from his own sometimes agonized experience of meditation (or *contemplation*):

> If such an 'I' one day hears about 'contemplation' he will perhaps set himself to 'become a contemplative'. That is, he will wish to admire in himself something called contemplation. And in order to see it, he will reflect on his alienated self. He will make contemplative faces at himself like a child in front of a mirror.

Merton can sometimes sound very harsh on himself (especially in his earlier writings) and it can feel like he's being harsh on you and me, his readers and would-be fellow meditators, as well. But in the end it is a loving warning about the dead ends that even something as spacious as meditation can turn into. If I have become acutely dissatisfied with who I am and the kind of life that I am leading, if all the routes that I choose keep turning out to be cul-de-sacs, then meditation and its teaching about the self seems to dangle an irresistible promise in front of me. Especially if I feel ravaged by a sense of wounding and grief that I just wish wasn't there and which I'd do anything to get rid of. It has blighted my life. That must be my depressed *false self*, right? Now all I have to do is to sit and become my *true* self, something much holier, more perfect. And if I practise really diligently I might even break through to the next level: no-self. All the pain can be left behind.

Something like this secret agenda of the ego is probably what brings most of us to meditation in the first place. The limited self wants to be less limited, more functional. It's an understandable project of self-improvement. But there are pitfalls waiting; sometimes taking up meditation can actually be a rush to appear whole or even holy (as much to ourselves as to others) rather than a commitment to the slow, steady and unglamorous work of becoming sane.

Ken Wilber, the celebrated American philosopher, has done more than most people over recent decades to promote the conversation between psychology, psychotherapy, spirituality and the practice of meditation. One of his core concepts helps us to understand what might be going on when we start to get confused about wholeness, holiness and sanity in our practice. He calls it the *pre/trans fallacy*. Wilber's model of consciousness is linked to a model of developmental psychology; it's also a model of the potential open to each human person. He distinguishes three fundamental categories: *pre-rational*; *rational* and *trans-rational* (sometimes also described as *pre-personal*, *personal* and *trans-personal*).

- *The pre-rational* designates the states of consciousness that we are involved in during the early stages of our lives: instinctive, mythic, primarily sensory, unconsciously unified with what surrounds us.
- In the *rational* category we have developed a sense of separate self; the mind and the intellect are navigating us, helping us to take our place in the agreed conventions of social and cultural life.
- Under the *trans-rational* category we are still body and mind (they are included) but we have found a way to expand into Self, a trans-personal,

fully conscious experience of connection with the totality of everything that is.

Wilber (a meditator) is critical of Freud, who seems to dismiss all expanded, 'oceanic' states of consciousness as just an infantile regression to a less developed state of being. He's equally critical of Jung, accusing him of elevating those pre-rational, early states of consciousness into a false equivalence with the trans-rational, which are by definition further evolved and more inclusive.

As we meditate our way through our depressions, Wilber's really helpful practical contribution is the encouragement to be awake to the difference between *pre-* and *trans-*. He draws our attention to that universal temptation to use 'spirituality' as another form of anaesthesia or dissociation when dealing with our wounding. If I go to enough retreats, sit as elegantly and steadfastly as possible, wrap myself each time in my special meditation blanket, then surely the pain will be dulled, surely I can cut off from the person I don't want to be or from the world which has caused me such suffering? In a way this is the limited self, the ego, wanting to jump all the way from *pre-* to *trans-* without taking each necessary (possibly boring and probably painful) step along the way of patient transformation. If the limited self sees another identity it likes the look of, and decides to do a swap, it is still, unfortunately, going to be the limited self. This is the *spiritual materialism* that wisdom teachers throughout the ages have warned us about. The *spiritual shortcut* is another of its names. It comes from our understandable rush to have our wounds healed as quickly and as elegantly as possible. It always reminds me of that lovable drunk in the cartoon, insisting on looking for his keys in the light and ignoring the darkness up the street, where he's just come from. *The light is better here.*

It seems like a trap. How are we ever going to escape from the empire of the limited self? If it is a trap, it's a benign one in the end. The good news is that the practice of meditation, faithfully followed, can itself release us from it. The deeply programmed strategy of every self (with a small 's') is to survive at all costs. It searches for yet more 'perfect' versions of itself, versions that it can take ever firmer possession of. The strategy is doomed; it will always end up by replacing one kind of loneliness with another. In searching for safety, the limited self accidentally finds more isolation. The gift of meditation is that it patiently exposes and exhausts this built-in tendency. The practice itself, with its simple and radical insistence on setting aside *all* thoughts, reminds us to let go of *any* new identity that we find ourselves about to grasp on to, no matter how 'holy' or 'contemplative'. This is the beginning of learning to see in the dark.

So the humble practice of meditation is appropriate at any stage in your life or in the waxing and waning of your sanity. You don't have to have spent years (and thousands of pounds) in therapy, getting a handle on all your 'pre-rational' material and issues, before you can announce yourself as 'rational' and therefore now ready to hit the meditation cushion and launch into the ocean of the 'trans-'. The practice of meditation is a generous discipline. Every part of everyone is welcome to be present. It teaches that healing is always a movement towards greater connection. It shows us that 'perfection' is not about being without fault, nor is it anything that can be achieved; it is simply an orientation, a fundamental openness. To what? To opening. And meditation reveals that if the *true self* is anything at all, it is never a possession but always a relationship.

We will almost certainly bring some old habits of splitting and dissociating with us into the meditation space. We want to be the best that we can be and we can't help having ideas about what that is. But judging and cutting off, no matter how elegantly done, is not the way *to leave self behind*. In fact, it has the reverse effect, entrapping us within an even more rigidly constructed version of the self. In Merton's words, this is 'altogether too much privacy'. After many struggles Merton discovered that wisdom is not wisdom if it only survives when you're alone. The same is true of sanity. We may have to spend a long time – like Merton – discovering what solitude is (completely different to privacy) and what healing is to be found there. But in the end we are called back into relationship, which is the heart of both holiness and sanity. It is not the opposite of solitude, but something that grows *out of* our chosen solitude. Like the ox-herder in the famous Ten Bulls sequence of Zen tradition, or like Jesus returning from the solitary wilderness, we come back to the marketplace, to others and to life. Everyday, messy, painful life and all the healing that waits for us there. Our solitude prepares us for it. *Meditation creates community.*

MEDITATION: WITH THE LEPER AND THE WOLF

Franciscan tradition tells us two stories that are a profound gift to every meditator and to every person tempted to escape his or her own darkness by fleeing into the supposed safety of a different, 'ideal' identity.

St Francis's signature is his empathy with the natural world and with animals in particular. For him it was instinctively *un*-natural to allow distance between himself and any part of creation. This is why the Sun was his brother and the Moon his sister. It's why he communed with the birds. He seemed to know at a cellular level that there was no such thing as being, only inter-being. He is someone for whom the only real sin is the refusal to connect with all the teeming manifestations of life; to stubbornly and defensively keep your distance. He doesn't want to leave anything out. This is the impulse that lies behind the story of his taming of a wolf, soon after his conversion. The people of Gubbio were terrorized by a huge, fierce and terrible beast which was preying on animals and humans alike. Everyone feared for their lives. Against all advice, Francis goes alone to meet the wolf, who runs towards him with slavering jaws.

The story tells us how Francis makes the sign of the cross and admonishes the beast, naming all the wrongs it has committed and the suffering it has caused. He offers to negotiate a peace with the people of the city, and the wolf – unused to being met and addressed – agrees. The citizens and their former enemy live in peaceful harmony for the next two years. They feed the wolf affectionately and mourn its passing when it dies.

The second celebrated story concerns another terror of the medieval mind: leprosy. Everybody avoided lepers, dreading the horrors that any contact with them would likely bring. The afflicted were forced to carry bells warning of their presence. They were explicitly cut off from the rest of humanity: rejected and excluded. Francis shared the general abhorrence for these outcasts, until the day when an inner prompting moves him to turn and face the leper he is about to ride away from. He dismounts, walks towards his greatest fear and embraces the man.

We're missing the deep personal significance of these stories for each one of us if we hear them merely as quaint fables or signs of 'miraculous' powers. At the heart of each transformative event is the steadfast intent *to enter into relationship*. To be whole, Francis knows that he must acknowledge the connection between himself, the wild beast and the weeping sores of the rejected one. He knows that separation – distance – is a false safety. It is leaving too much out.

We all have a version of both the leper and the wolf woven into our stories and our sense of who we think we are (and who we often insist we *aren't*). We may have a sense of what they stand for; we may even perhaps be able to provide some names. It might simply be the thing that we call 'my' depression or 'my' anxiety. Or maybe some more specific names: anger, shame, fear, guilt, abuse, addiction, violence, never-ending grief ... Or it may just be a general but potent sense that I am somehow simply not good enough. In every case, both the leper and the wolf stand for that which I have decided is unacceptable about me. These are the things that I want to deny, leave behind, or – at the very least – change.

Following that path may bring a brief appearance of (pseudo-)holiness, but there will be no sanity. Because actually your sanity is already here, waiting for you. And it is not 'your' sanity, although it lies at the irreducible core of your being. Nor is it inaccessibly buried only in your depths – the core is everywhere and always available. All you have to do is to have the steadfast intention to be as fully present as you can be during your time of meditation. Almost certainly, this will involve taking a few breaths while you courageously acknowledge the lepers and wolves that you have been holding, and are still holding, at bay. Name them, if you can. If you can't, it will be powerful enough to see the leper and the wolf and to invite them to sit with you, next to your meditation cushion or your chair. Make sure you make room for them. Sit with your wounding and your wildness. You can't be in relationship with them if they're not here. If they are, then the complete surrender – the un-naming – can start straight away, and continue with each breath, each sounding of the mantra. Expose your *entire* being to the radiance of the present moment. This is the real miracle.

Before meditation:

If anyone wishes to be a follower of mine, he must leave self behind.

Meditate for 20 minutes

After meditation:

> *O housebuilder, now you are seen!*
> *You will not build the house again:*
> *all your rafters have been broken,*
> *and the ridgepole has been destroyed.*

LIFE IS THE TREATMENT!

In 1992 – the same year that I went to America and learned from Jim Finley how to keep on beginning to meditate – I found myself making an information video with users of mental health services. I was working for a voluntary organization called Mental Health Media. I was fascinated to discover that it had been set up in 1963 as The Mental Health Film Council. The year of its establishment was significant. A group of concerned individuals connected with Mind, the mental health charity, were disturbed by the effect that the filmed assassination of the American president might have on the mental wellbeing of the public. It sounds quaint now, a good intention doomed to being swept away by the tidal wave of horrifying (and then numbing) images that the future was to become. And all only a click away. The concern, though, was justified and also commendable. Instead of having that grotesque Zapruder footage constantly playing on a loop in our heads (something that YouTube effortlessly facilitates 55 years later), wasn't there some more positive use to which we could put all this burgeoning technology? Something that would actually help our mental health?

Which is how I came to be standing on a sunlit street in Leicester, about to interview Michael, who identified as a survivor of mental health services. I was directing and producing a video called *From Anger to Action*. What excited me most about this piece of work was that my editorial group – the people that I was answerable to – all identified as 'experts by experience'. They had all at one time or another in their lives been given a mental health diagnosis (including severe depression) and had experienced psychiatric treatment. In this video – a follow-up to an earlier TV programme, *We're Not Mad, We're Angry* – they were saying just what it was that they hadn't liked about this treatment. More than that, they were desperate to say what it was that they *did* find helpful and what they wished they'd been offered when they first became unwell. Their wish list is quite easy to sum up and sounds entirely reasonable – and sane: empathy and understanding; someone to listen non-judgementally to their distress; places of safety when necessary; the option of informed choice around treatment (including access to complementary therapies); the opportunity to engage in meaningful activity (paid and unpaid); friendship and support from individuals, groups and community; and the confidence that they would be respected as whole persons, rather than dealt with as just 'patients' or 'problems'.

Michael was a volunteer at a community-based resource, situated on the corner of a street in the heart of the local community. It was run entirely by people who had lived experience of mental health difficulties. He was also a gift to the anxious director/interviewer, who wanted to make sure that the message came over loud and clear. I had been hoping, at the least, for usable sound-bites. Michael went way beyond that and provided words that had the clarity and force of *haiku*. Talking about his vision of how we can best respond to each other's emotional distress, he said this: 'In the old days you were sent away to hospital for treatment. But people have to live – life is the treatment!'

I've remained grateful to Michael over many years. In those four words he summed up an approach to human misery that was in danger then – as it still is now – of being overlooked. It happens whenever we fall into the temptation of over-medicalizing our response to people's losses and griefs. Michael was giving voice to an obvious truth which at that point was barely acknowledged by the medical (and particularly the psychiatric) establishment. Since then, the common-sense power of the insight has asserted itself, giving rise about fifteen years ago to what became known as the Recovery Approach. At the heart of this approach is the fundamental assertion that not only is there a way back from mental and emotional distress, no matter how severe, but there is also a way *through* it – a way that can bring enhanced self-knowledge and increased resilience. Properly understood, the Recovery Approach gives us the encouraging news that our recovery can be an unexpected and blessed process of *discovery* as well.

The Recovery Approach is also, essentially, a whole-person approach. Brilliantly summed up by Michael's four-word mantra, it recognizes that conditions such as anxiety and depression, post-traumatic stress disorder, phobias, self-harming and psychosis are not *exclusively* medical conditions. Nor, of course, are any other illnesses, which may be much more obviously physical in nature and even have identifiable pathologies. All illness, of whatever kind, takes place in the context of a person's whole life. It seems a blindingly obvious statement to make, but it acts as a necessary reminder that experiences of ill-health are not only managed, treated and recovered from in the consulting room or the hospital, but in the multi-faceted space that is your life and my life.

The day after the attack on the World Trade Center in 2001, I started my job as the manager of a new mental health and wellbeing project run by Mind in Norwich. We had recognized that our services, along with all the other available services in the city, had long been besieged by people whose lives had been arrested and thrown off course by experiences that it was easiest to describe as depression and anxiety. But the current services had no spare capacity with which to respond to these people's lostness and anguish. All resources were used up in dealing with people described as having 'severe and enduring' mental health problems. Anyone who has felt the malevolent and fierce numbness of a depression for any length of time will tell you that it definitely feels 'severe and enduring'. But these were the experiences that were not being catered for, beyond the possibility of a short encounter with a GP and a prescription of the latest wonder-drug such as Seroxat or Prozac.

We decided to make available – perhaps foolishly – a resource called Mind, Body & Soul, to which people could self-refer either by telephone, email or simply by walking in. *Perhaps foolishly*, because, of course, we were very soon flooded with a level of requests that it was difficult for us to meet. What was on offer was an initial meeting (which we deliberately didn't call an *assessment*) in a light and comfortable room where someone would be listened to with full, non-judging attention. In that session we would offer reassurance, information and the possibility of a referral-on to our small team of in-house counsellors and complementary therapists. We were completely committed to the Recovery Approach, before it had even been named as that. Over a number of years I conducted most of those initial meetings. I would say that at least 90 per cent of the people who came to us had been given a diagnosis of depression or described themselves as 'depressed'.

I was always moved – and found it poignant – to see just what an enormous effect it often had on people simply to be listened to. Sitting down for a full hour, in an environment that we made as beautiful as possible, it was clear that for many this was the first time it had happened. It was a gentle shock for them to be invited to 'say as much or as little' as they would like to about what was going on for them at this point in their lives. Over and over again we felt the powerful impact of the question that released the Fisher King and his frozen wasteland: 'What ails thee, friend?'

After a while, I began to notice a pattern, even a rhythm, that kept emerging in these sessions. Almost always, after our latest visitor had talked at length about the pain or despair or bewilderment that he or she was feeling, there would come a lull and a moment when I found myself asking: 'What do you enjoy?' Or: 'What keeps you going?' Of course, in the context of all that misery, the question risks being answered with a defeated 'Nothing' or 'I don't know'. But usually the mere fact of having named the misery would open up an unexpected space. If I was patient or encouraging enough, the person with me would nearly always come up with something: 'Well, there's my cat', or 'I couldn't manage without my yoga class', or 'I used to edit a lot of music on my computer', or 'My children', or 'Going for walks', or 'My garden', or 'Reading', or 'I like to keep a journal, but I've stopped now ...'

There's one man I remember very clearly. A builder, middle-aged, stocky and gentle, with close-cropped hair, always neatly turned out. The world would immediately recognize him as a 'good family man', a dependable, solid, honest citizen. For no reason that was obvious to him, for the first time in his life, he had become gradually overtaken by a creeping sense of terror. So much so that he didn't recognize himself. The members of his family seemed like strangers to him, and his own body, suddenly weak, fragile and trembling, was an alien being. He was deeply ashamed that he was barely able to carry on with his daily work of being the dependable strong man. He was beside himself. When we reached *that point* in our initial meeting and I asked him if there was anything that brought him any kind of relief, no matter how short-lived, he talked about his fishing. It was something that he'd done on and off all his life, but at that moment it was as if this was all he was able to do. He wept as he described it: how he felt a tiny modicum of safety as he sat still and in silence (he went fishing by himself) at the water's edge. I encouraged him to do it as much as he wanted, and for as long as he wanted. I had a strong image of him sitting there, fishing for his life. And, yes, I thought about the Fisher King. In the meantime, we set up some appointments for him to see one of our in-house counsellors.

I came to regard this pivot-point in the initial meetings as a sacred moment. It was the point at which the person clearly had a choice: whether to acknowledge that, yes, there was something, or someone, that still provided them with some kind of connection, or at least the memory of a connection, with something other than the prison that their own experience had become. Movingly, nearly always this was the choice that was made, rather than the bleak denial of any contact at all with the 'outside world' and the life that waited there. Perhaps these were real glimpses of what Simone Weil said lay at the bottom of the heart of every human being: the lingering expectation, despite all the evidence, 'that good and not evil will be done to him'. And her.

Gwyneth Lewis says, about her own experience of depression, that it was her poetry that kept her alive. Miraculously, apart from the most overwhelmingly intense times of emotional and physical paralysis, her ability to reflect her experience by playing with words and lines didn't desert her. In *Sunbathing in the Rain* she fervently wishes that her readers will find their own 'poetry' to sustain them, to keep them connected. The connecting thread can be the slenderest of lines, like a line of verse, or the wispy filament that runs from the end of a fishing rod, but it is still a lifeline. What Gwyneth is pointing to when she encourages us to find our own poetry is the healing power (and this is the only place, in the end, where that power resides) of *staying in relationship*. Only connect.

As I reflected on what these slender connecting threads meant in a person's life, I saw what, at heart, they all were. The cat, the music, the fishing, the yoga, the abandoned writing, the garden – they were all a release from the crushing imprisonment of self-obsession. All of these activities, which in truth were actually relationships, *took people out of themselves*. Sometimes the most banal of phrases conceals the deepest truths. When people were engaged in these activities and these relationships, they were freed for a time from the confines of a self that seemed to be made up of nothing but restless complexity and mute noise. Because their attention was placed somewhere other than on themselves and their suffering (the black hole that threatens to let nothing get out), they were more available to life and to the treatment it has to offer.

When I thought in such terms about these vital threads that our visitors bravely volunteered, I started to realize what they had in common with the practice of meditation that I was still beginning over and over again. I had begun to understand meditation as prayer – the silent prayer of the heart, as Christian contemplatives have long described it. More than this, I had begun to understand prayer as nothing to do with asking for things or even fervently wishing for good things to happen. That had long seemed to be just more daydreaming. Prayer is the simple act of choosing to place your attention elsewhere, away from the busy and obsessive agendas of the self. Prayer, in the end, in the beginning, and at all points in between, is simply the humble readiness to be in relationship with something that is not yourself, with the *other*.

If that is the heart of prayer, a trust that enables you to turn away from complete fixation with the self, then I began to see that prayer could be everywhere, and everything could be prayer. Dancing, listening to music, digging a flowerbed, building a model boat, risking an evening class, reading, walking, sitting for hours (even days) by the water and never catching anything – all of these are forms of living prayer. If they *take you out of yourself* and put you, no matter how fleetingly, into relationship with something *other*, there will always be a taste of stillness, simplicity and silence about it. That is the fundamental nature of true relationship and of the treatment that life has to offer. It's why fishing, walking the dog or seeing what you can develop in the dark room are all sacred – and potentially healing – moments.

TREATING EACH OTHER

'The way we treat each other is the treatment.' These are the words of the celebrated psychiatrist Ronnie Laing. They are worthy of being put alongside those of Michael (*Life is the treatment!*) as a summary of how we help each other over and over again back to sanity. Laing was talking in one of the last interviews he gave before his death. He went on to assert that it was the quality of attention that we are prepared to give to the other that is the true therapy. We tried to model this at Mind, Body & Soul in the way we met people, how we listened to them, and in the kind of information and support that we provided. I'd like to offer some of that practical guidance to you now.

As I've described, I would always encourage someone to cultivate whatever it was that provided some measure of relief or even just the faintest flicker of continued meaning in his or her life. But engaging in activity or being in any kind of relationship is often exactly what someone experiencing crushing anguish feels they are incapable of. Before they can begin to remember that Life is indeed the Treatment, something else needs to happen. It's what we repeatedly witnessed and took part in at Mind, Body

& Soul: the acknowledging and the naming of a person's pain. Whether it was called depression or anxiety, grief or loneliness, addiction or despair, the key event was that it was named and shared. In many ways the importance of such a transaction is that it is a *rite of passage*. It recognizes that you are in a transition of some kind and that you deserve to be cared for and encouraged to take good care of yourself. At its most compassionate this is the honouring of the vulnerable body of the crab as it moves agonizingly from one temporary shelter to the next. At its clumsiest it can turn into what Laing himself described psychiatric intervention as all too often becoming: *a humiliation ritual*.

When anyone asks me what they can do about their feelings of lostness, panic, despair, self-hatred or overwhelming sadness, there are specific professional practitioners that I suggest they might consider going to see in the first instance: doctors and counsellors or psychotherapists. These are vital points of contact, providing places where you can at last (in confidence) go public by beginning to give voice to your pain. The rite of passage can potentially begin with GPs, as they are the providers of medication, access to secondary services and – in recent decades – other forms of treatment such as exercise on prescription or bibliotherapy (books for wellbeing).

DOCTORS

General practitioners are usually overworked and short on time. Nevertheless, I have met doctors who have been enormously generous with both their time and the quality of their attention. I have felt the truth of Ronnie Laing's simple insight. No matter what kind of complaint I have gone in with, just being treated that way has made me walk out of the surgery feeling much better. I have also had the experience of talking to the side of a doctor's face as he or she taps urgently at a computer keyboard, obviously intent on printing out a prescription as quickly as possible and moving on to the next patient. Unsurprisingly, my sense of being alone with my problem has intensified. I pray that the doctor you go to see is someone who is able to see you and connect with you and who remembers that your life continues way beyond the ten minutes of your allotted encounter.

If your doctor decides that your diagnosis is depression or anxiety or some combination of the two (perhaps mixed in with other conditions), he or she will almost certainly offer you antidepressant medication. The use – and the effectiveness – of antidepressants is controversial, as we've touched on in an earlier section of this book. The controversy around this form of treatment continues. In February of 2018 a report was published in the leading medical journal, *The Lancet*, announcing the results of a six-year study which had looked at over five hundred clinical trials involving a range of antidepressants. The story was featured in the *Guardian* newspaper under the headline: 'The drugs do work: antidepressants are effective, study shows'. The subheadings elaborate on what outcomes the proponents of these medications were looking for:

Doctors hope study will put to rest doubts about the medicine, and help to address global under-treatment of depression

It's official: antidepressants are not snake oil or a conspiracy

Their hopes may or may not have been fulfilled. The expected counter-arguments came swiftly, with sceptics pointing out flaws in the methodology of the research, as well as drawing attention to the often under-reported side-effects of antidepressants, which can include sexual dysfunction, permanently dry mouth, lassitude and emotional blunting. Some also raised the obvious question: if antidepressants are as effective as they are claimed to be, how come the prevalence of depression is still rising at an alarming rate? Their opponents would answer in turn that depression is simply being *under-treated*. More prescriptions need to be written for more people. 'But would this be addressing the real problems?' comes back the question from others, including Joanna Moncrieff, a psychiatrist, who remains keenly aware of the limitations of antidepressants. She points out how they have no effect on the many factors that are contributing to people finding it more and more difficult to cope with life, including 'insecure or inadequate employment, finances and housing, loneliness, increasing pressure to perform and reach ever higher targets at work and school, loss of meaning in life and the disappearing nature of community in many areas'.

How to decide if medication is for you? Experience is the teacher and information is power. You don't know until you've tried, but you don't know if you want to try unless you are given an informed choice. It is your doctor's responsibility to explain to you how it is believed that antidepressants work, what sort of time-frame is being suggested, as well as covering all the pros and cons of using this kind of medication. It's important that this is done in a face-to-face, open-ended conversation. It's not enough to leave you simply reading the increasingly newspaper-sized list of information and advice enclosed in each packet of your drugs.

I have never taken an antidepressant, so I can't speak with personal authority about the experience of using this medication. I can only report that I have met and spoken with some people who feel that they have been helped by the tablets that they have been prescribed and who are grateful to have been offered them. I also know many people who have told me that they haven't felt at all helped, that in fact their misery intensified. I'm sorry I can't give any clearer guidance than that. Inform yourself as much as you can; speak, if possible, to people who have experience, who know what they're talking about. (Medication seems to have a particularly important role to play if the diagnosis is 'bipolar disorder' – what used to be called manic depression. Again, it's vital that you, or someone caring for you, are both enabled to make an informed choice).

What I *do* know is that it is also the responsibility of every GP to not *just* offer antidepressants. I hope that it is now much less likely that this will happen than even, say, 15 years ago. The idea of Recovery – that Life is the Treatment – has steadily permeated the collective consciousness, including that of the medical providers. GPs, for instance, are now increasingly offering 'social prescribing', giving people access to activities such as volunteering, the arts, gardening, befriending, healthy eating advice and a range of exercise options.

Doctors are also the people who can offer you some time to recover in hospital. Put as simply as that, it sounds like an utterly benign opportunity. Of course the situation is much more problematic if the hospital or therapeutic unit doesn't seem to offer what you need at this tender and frightening moment in your life. It becomes even more so if you are adamant that you don't want to go to hospital, while those who are offering you support are advising – even insisting – that you should. We're touching here on immense ethical, legal and clinical issues that will continue to be contested, and rightly so. They can only ever be provisionally negotiated in each particular instance – in the specific circumstances of every unique life at that given moment.

The only practical advice that I feel moved to offer here concerns how we think about hospitals. A default position for individuals or families often is to believe that *going into hospital* is somehow the end of the road or a cause for shame. We need to remember (and this includes those working there and managing services) that a hospital should at heart be *a place of safety* and therefore a place of hope. When *psych-iatry* has not forgotten the meaning of its profession (from Greek, *the healing of souls*), this is precisely what a hospital can be. Of course, I have seen all too often the heartbreaking inadequacies of services on offer in localities where I have worked, with lack of resources and unsupported staff a recurrent theme. But I have also seen many people, including dear friends and members of my own family, held in the therapeutic embrace of a truly caring community while they recover, discover and come back to themselves, renewed.

In *Darkness Visible*, William Styron writes movingly about the vital role that his time in hospital played in his recovery. He expresses immense gratitude for the refuge and asylum that his stay allowed him to experience. The bruised mind and the broken heart simply needed time to be allowed to stop, to be cared for, to wait and to heal. When hospitals enable this to happen – and they often do – they are honouring their historic origins. The very first 'infirmaries' were an essential part of all early monasteries, where the healing environment was the daily rhythm of chanted and silent prayer, the fellowship of the community and the deep conviction that the leper, the wanderer, the poor and the lost were all beloved of Christ:

> For I was hungry and you gave me something to eat, I was thirsty and you gave me something to drink, I was a stranger and you invited me in, I needed clothes and you clothed me, I was sick and you looked after me, I was in prison and you came to visit me.

One of the most important things that doctors are increasingly able to do is to give you access – sometimes in hospital, but much more usually outside of it – to 'talking treatments': counselling and psychotherapy.

TALKING THERAPIES

'What ails thee, friend?' is the question that underpins every relationship with a therapist or counsellor. We all have a story to tell about how we got to this point, but most of us consciously know only part of the story. Some of us, understandably, have done everything possible to avoid the entire story – it is simply too painful. The psychotherapist is there to help us discover what has shaped us, what has limited us, and to remind us of our enormous potential to grow beyond those painful and – in the end – illusory limits. Once again it involves the patience and the courage to name and then rename aspects of your own experience. The therapeutic encounter offers the potential for you to re-author your life, liberating yourself from all the old stories, imposed by others and by the dead weight of unexplored events. It is an opportunity to become more authentic – more like *you*.

What's the difference between counselling and psychotherapy? The traditional answer would be that counselling is likely to be something that happens over a shorter period of time, which focuses more on the here and now, rather than exploring your past and your unconscious memories. Actually, the distinction between psychotherapy and counselling is difficult to make and, increasingly perhaps, not worth the effort. What is universally acknowledged is that it is the quality of the relationship between client and therapist that is key in opening up a space where healing can take place.

Looking for a therapist can be a bewildering proposition, especially if you find yourself in a state of mind in which it seems impossible to make any kind of decision or to feel any measure of trust that the next step you take in your life won't bring just more disappointment, or worse, disaster. I'd always want to reassure someone in this position that the very desire to seek help is itself a sure indication of a healing that is ready to take place. It's a glimpse of that 'brilliant sanity' spoken of by Buddhist practitioners, a brilliant sanity wanting to manifest itself in the here and now. This sanity is our essential quality, always present at our core, patiently waiting to flood through us and to help us see better in the dark. To allow it to expand we need to stop (or, sometimes, *be* stopped – by life, perhaps by 'depression'), to sit still and find someone we trust to be alongside us as we explore.

It's useful to know the outlines of the different approaches to counselling and psychotherapy. In practice, more and more therapists will have an eclectic understanding, borrowing from across a number of the traditions. Broadly, the different approaches are:

Psychoanalytic and Psychodynamic: These are associated with the teachings of the founders of psychotherapy, such as Freud and Jung. Typically these ways of working concentrate on exploring the unconscious content of the psyche – what you have forgotten you have forgotten – helping you to see whatever it is that is driving you or limiting you and causing you misery. The understanding is that whatever is brought to consciousness will no longer have such devastating power over you. Often these therapeutic relationships can extend over a considerable period of time.

Person-centred and Humanistic: These emphasize the quality of the relationship between therapist and client as a key enabler for change. Such approaches explicitly honour each person's innate wisdom and desire for health, balance and integration. Within these traditions there is sometimes a readiness to incorporate bodywork (massage, gentle movement, focusing etc.), recognizing that there can be no integration without the inclusion of our physical being and the wisdom that it embodies.

Cognitive behavioural therapy (CBT): This is the form of talking treatment that you are most likely to be offered by your doctor. It has become popular within the National Health Service in recent years for a number of reasons. One of these is that it promises, and can sometimes deliver, relatively quick and measurable outcomes in terms of changed behaviour and a shift in someone's understanding of themselves, their habits and patterns of thinking. Over the past decade in particular, CBT has been increasingly recognized as an effective way to respond to people describing the kind of experiences that lead to the diagnosis of depression or anxiety. The National Institute for Health and Care Excellence (Nice) has given its approval. In the UK, GPs are now able to refer you through a programme called IAPT (Increased Access to Psychological Therapies) to a course of cognitive behavioural therapy. Many more people are taking up the offer. Across 2016–17 there were 1.39 million new IAPT referrals.

Some have expressed reservations about the nature of the changed perspectives offered by CBT. How profound and lasting can any shifts be, they ask, which concentrate only on the thoughts in our head ('cognitive') and our resulting behaviour? What about those other repositories of human mystery, human suffering and human joy – the heart, the body, the soul? In many ways some of those criticisms have been answered by the meeting in recent years between mindfulness and CBT. Mindfulness is a form of meditation practice which shares some common ground with meditation as understood and described in this book. It also has some significant differences (see below). Courses in mindfulness-based CBT (MCBT) have now been approved by Nice and are increasingly available – sometimes by prescription via your doctor – throughout the UK.

If CBT is the form of talking treatment you are offered by your doctor in the UK, it will be accessible via the National Health Service without payment. The other 'modalities', as they're sometimes called, are most often available on a private paying basis, though there is a possibility of sliding scales, especially when the therapy is being offered by a mental health organization such as Mind or a charity-funded counselling centre.

How to choose someone? Personal recommendation remains the best way; it's a real blessing if a friend or even a friend of a friend is able suggest a therapist or counsellor to work with, based on good personal experience. If that isn't the case, there are certificating bodies who hold the registrations of professionally accredited practitioners. In the United Kingdom these are the UKCP and the BACP. Looking at their websites or ringing their information service is the best way to start this potentially life-changing relationship.

Remember: therapists are not omniscient, nor are they perfect or perfectly wise. (Of course – without giving too much of the game away – learning this very truth might itself be the beginning of you accessing, and living from, your own always-available wisdom.) Therapists can make mistakes and some will inevitably be people who, for one reason or another, you just can't get on with. These blockages and resistances can themselves sometimes be the source of painful learning and new self-knowledge. But sometimes it just means that you're with the wrong therapist. In which case, please try again – don't give up. This is a time when you are likely to be feeling great vulnerability and hopelessness. The temptation not to take any kind of risk is completely understandable. But I urge you to trust that there *will* be someone whose patient offer of accompaniment, insight and compassionate listening is just right – or right *enough* – for you. Because, whatever happens, and no matter how tireless and how committed your therapist is to your wellbeing, it will always be YOU who is the one doing the real transformative work, which is exactly what will make it so valuable and irreplaceable in your life.

There's lots of other work that we can be doing as well, to help us through depression and to learn from it. I'll say a little more about one or two of the activities we can engage in. They all have something in common: at heart they are all the kind of work that teaches us to be more *playful*.

MOVEMENT

One of the most positive developments to have emerged from the Recovery Approach to mental and emotional distress is the extent to which the health of our bodies is now taken to be an essential part of the whole picture. All forms of sport and exercise, from full-out sprinting to gentle strolling, plus every imaginable team and individual activity in between, are known to be powerful ways of changing our moods and maintaining wellbeing. Feel-good endorphins are released, there is the potential for contact with others, our attention is placed elsewhere, we discover – or invent – some temporary purpose in a day that otherwise feels oppressively meaningless.

For me it has been badminton – a sport I am not particularly good at, but which I am able to launch myself into with an enthusiastic abandon that is liberating. In a noisy sports hall the shuttlecock becomes a kind of mantra. (But only in retrospect – as I write about it. At the time the shuttlecock is – as it must be – just a shuttlecock.) I'm sure the same can be true about the golf ball, the horizon you are jogging towards, the tennis ball, the slowly nearing end of the swimming lane in front of you, the football, the sea that is going to deliver the next perfect wave that you and your board are going to catch. They are all mantras of a kind, helping your scattered mind to clarify and to settle – and they are also exactly just what they are in that unrepeatable moment of attention.

The benefits of losing (and finding) ourselves in activities such as these are both experientially and scientifically verifiable. It makes great sense and it's self-evident. This is why exercise on prescription is proving so popular, whether people have mental or physical health issues. The point, of course, is that they always have both.

Taking part in sport or going to the gym is 'exercise', but exercise is only part of something more fundamental, which is *movement*. Not everyone is able, or chooses, to take part in such energetic activities. There are gentler movements we can invite our bodies to make, ones that let go of points scored and personal bests set (those can be fun too). Yoga, tai chi, qigong, dance – these are all ways that we can start to be playful again with our bodies, releasing the long-held tensions and blockages where we have buried the distress of our lives. And it's a different kind of movement to the increasingly mechanical gestures with which we get through our days: dashing in and out of a car with children, clicking a mouse thousands of times before you've even had lunch, running for a train ... These become deeply grooved habits which trap our energy and stifle all creativity. They form the *business* of getting through our lives – quite different to the rediscovery of playful movement.

Is gardening exercise? That's one of its aspects. Is it movement? It certainly involves a lot of purposeful and attentive physical activity. Surely it's both of these, and more besides. Cultivating a relationship with the earth under our feet is always a connection with mystery and a lesson in patience. Whether you're involved in a conservation project, tending a vegetable patch or looking after a window-box and some pots on the balcony of your flat, your attention has moved out beyond the confines of the running commentary that all too often fills the whole of our experience. Planting, feeding, nurturing, harvesting, you are cooperating with the fundamental rhythms of life. Holding a trowel, a packet of seeds and some pots filled with compost, you are an intimate part of THE great mystery of growth, death and regrowth. There could be no more immediate teacher. What is happening in plain view, and in the shoots and soil between our fingers, is what is also happening in us. No wonder that the Upanishads take the tiniest of seeds as the image of 'the Spirit that is in my heart, greater than the earth, greater than the sky, greater than heaven itself'. No wonder that the language of farming and gardening provides so many of the powerful images in Jesus' teaching. The seed is never far from his parables. The kingdom, he says, is like this:

A man scatters seed on the land; he goes to bed at night and gets up in the morning, and the seed sprouts and grows – how, he does not know.

Zen notices the same growth in silent astonishment. Its approach to gardening is even less hands-on. As the Zen proverb says, 'Sitting quietly, doing nothing, spring comes, and the grass grows by itself.'

We *do not know how* this happens. We can only witness and celebrate in silent astonishment. But we can also know that we are intimately bound into this mystery. Here is a profound movement that is not part of our planning, nor is it one that we can control. We can, though, participate in it, if we are prepared to move at a different pace, one that the urgent demands of the ego might not even recognize as movement at all. It's a significant shift: the difference between standing apart from life and entering into it. Getting our hands healthily dirty, as we move downwards with the roots and outwards with the branches.

It's the same sense of movement that underpins some of the helpful formulas for wellbeing that have emerged in recent years. Ten years ago The New Economics Foundation built on the Recovery Approach to offer its Five Ways to Wellbeing, which are now also promoted by the NHS:

- Connect
- Be active
- Keep learning
- Give
- Take notice and be mindful

That's exactly what I can't do, says depression – *I'm depressed!* That may seem true at the time. It's also true that choosing to keep these encouraging signposts in sight will surely build our resilience and sustain our growth. Following these clues, we may not need to spend so much time in a state of depression. Our mourning and our learning can go hand in hand.

Also, you don't have to learn to play an instrument, join a support group, go running every day, volunteer at the local hospital, sign up for an evening class – and more – all at once. If there is just *one* connection, then follow that, no matter how humble or fragile it may seem at the time: simply listening to music, walking the dog, reading, working with a complementary therapist, cooking and eating healthily for the first time in a long while, or simply sitting and watching the grass grow by itself. In astonishment, if that comes. All of these activities, entered into with a growing trust in life itself as the treatment, offer a movement that is quite different from the restlessness, the hyper-activity and the fruitless repetitions that come from our distress. The movement can become the movement of mutual relationship and patient growth. For that to be the case, we have to relearn a forgotten way of moving, one that has stillness at its heart. As T. S. Eliot says, 'We must be still and still moving.'

MEDITATION

I can think of few better descriptions of meditation in the face of depression (and at all other times) than the great poet's line above, from 'East Coker' in *Four Quartets*. Especially as he goes on to say,

Into another intensity
For a further union, a deeper communion
Through the dark cold and empty desolation ...

For meditation as 'treatment' and much more than treatment, see all of the rest of this book. But I couldn't leave it out of this section; I wanted to name it as a fundamental orientation and as a practice that can underpin all of the rest of your life and your treatment. It's also an opportunity to be quite clear that it is never a question, for instance, of meditation OR medication. I know many people – and have been in touch with some in the course of writing this book – who do both. There is no contradiction and no contra-indication. Meditation and medication are doing very different things, but they can both be part of your treatment, understood in the widest possible sense. As I've said, I can't speak from personal experience about antidepressants in particular. I can say, though, that meditation is voluntary and free. It opens the way to friendship and community, and the only 'side-effects' that I have ever experienced have been entirely wonderful.

Including it briefly in this section is also a chance to put meditation alongside mindfulness for a moment. Mindfulness has become widely popularized in the past decade. It is a practice that is adapted from the original tradition of Buddhist insight meditation. It is becoming increasingly taught in schools, in the workplace and even in institutions such as parliament and the military. More often than not, mindfulness is presented as a secular practice, something ancient that has been made contemporary 'for our busy times'.

Wisdom is still wisdom, and is still operative, in the setting of mindfulness courses and practice. The rebranding exercise which made mindfulness available to the world has indeed given a great gift to a great many. Since Jon Kabat-Zinn started offering Mindfulness-based Stress Reduction courses in Boston in 1979, countless people around the world have found the beginnings of a new way to hold and to release the pain that comes with anxiety and depression. Meditation as I practise it, and as I try to present it in this book, shares a great deal with mindfulness. The silent, attentive moment remains the silent attentive moment, whatever name the practice might temporarily have borrowed. But meditation can go further than Mindfulness. Whether it is Taoist, Sufi, Hindu, Buddhist, Christian or something beyond all of these names, it offers a way of union. The self is experienced as intimately participating in a greater Self which is both within and beyond, and therefore shared at a deep level of communion with all other beings. Experienced in this way, meditation reveals itself as prayer: the movement towards unity in love, in which you are as much attended to as attending, in the stillness, simplicity and silence.

Taken together – the healing that life itself can be, the patient friendship of others, the transformative care of attentive professionals, along with the ability that meditation brings to wait through both hope and despair – all of this can be the gentle kind of holding that we need at times of vulnerability and transition. What it can provide is a vehicle, or a home, within which you are able to be depressed – which might mean in mourning – for *exactly as long as you need to be*, no longer and no shorter. Then, changed, you are brought back to life, which is change itself.

MEDITATION: A PERPETUAL SURPRISE

That I exist is a perpetual surprise which is life.

Rabindranath Tagore

What is it to be fully alive? All the wisdom traditions make it clear that it is not to do with a heroic accumulation of experience and achievement. It is not about the temporary rush that 'winning' brings, despite what the ego, the World (and some of its leaders) all seem to believe. The wisdom teachers bear witness to a different truth, one that we have to relearn over and over: that fullness of life lies outside the fortress of the limited self. The purpose of our lives is quite simply to avoid being *full of ourselves*. Making ourselves *bigger*, *better* and *safer* won't work: we need to make room for the life-giving connection with the other. The creation of such room will always feel like a loss to the limited self, the one that wants to stay in control at all costs. It will feel like death.

The limited self tries to be alive in the only way it knows: defending, impressing, hiding, constantly checking and comparing. Trying this hard squeezes the life out of life. We need to try not to try so hard. The paradox will feel like another dead end unless we have a practice – something that we can *actually do* – which makes a reality of it, in your life and my life, here and now. This is why it helps to understand the practice of meditation as *giving up without giving up*. The clenched and exhausting effort to succeed is surrendered. You give up the intense activity of unrelenting self-creation. You open to the presence of those spaces in you and around you that no one possesses. They are not *you*, they are not the *other*: they are simply the ground where you and the other meet, without the need to name and divide.

These openings in the fortress of the self can feel like invasion or decay. And they will keep on feeling, at times, like death. Every wisdom teaching from every tradition, in one way or another, patiently offers us the great central lesson: that to live fully we *must die before we die*. Perhaps many, many times. This is the true meaning of *giving up without giving up*. We have to find a way of repeatedly shedding the incomplete versions of ourselves that up to then we had taken as the Finished Article. There is no such thing. And remember the fundamental insight that there are only two agents of profound transformation in our lives: suffering and prayer. They both create holes in the self's defences – or perhaps expose the gaps in what we had hoped was so complete. But they also open the way for our growth.

What if the suffering that we call depression contains experiences and lessons without which we cannot be fully alive? At the time of the seemingly unbearable pain, it seems like a scandalous, even a heartless, suggestion. But bringing our suffering into our prayer – sitting through our depression in meditation – is a way of doing the dying that we need to do, before we die. The one effort that we are required to make is to stop trying to be alive in the same old way. Opening to this moment, stripped of everything except the mantra and the breath, is how we are made and unmade, how we grow and live.

Before meditation:

I have come that you may have life, and have it in all its fullness.

John 10.10

Meditate for 20 minutes

After meditation:

When making your choice in life, do not neglect to live.

Samuel Johnson

INTO THE DESERT

The world is too much with us; late and soon,
Getting and spending, we lay waste our powers.

William Wordsworth

There are many kinds of deserts. The familiar image of the physical desert is of an arid landscape parched by the relentless burning heat of the sun. It is an empty place and a place, above all, devoid of anything that will sustain life. With its searing exposure and its absence of water and shelter, the desert threatens emergency at all times. For many people, at a certain point in their life, the whole world will turn into a desert. 'The world' is then not so much a location as a way of being and a state of mind.

It is all too easy to be anaesthetized into believing that 'the world' as presented to you is the only one there is; and that the role set out for you is the one you have no choice but to follow. Industrial and post-industrial culture encourages each of us to exist primarily as producers and consumers. The arrival of social media and an entire cyber-sphere has elaborated this given reality and found ways to deliver it ever more intimately and convincingly. Now we are not just producers and consumers; with the remorseless harvesting of our attention and our data, we are the product as well. Not only that, we are now all both entertainers and the entertained – and we are entertaining ourselves to death. If you are lucky you will wake up before that vanishing point arrives, to find yourself unsheltered from the relentless sun and surrounded by sand as far as the eye can see.

The shocking discovery that your world has become a desert is the necessary first step towards healing. The deception is no longer working. No matter how many bright and shiny objects are dangled in front of you, on- or off-line, this world is no longer enough for you. It acknowledges your existence and demands your attention and participation, but it knows nothing of *your life*. Why not? Because 'the world' understood in this way is a habitual construct, thrown up by our conditioning, our fears and our desires. It's one that the 'attention merchants' (Google, Facebook, Twitter, the usual suspects) are expert at reinforcing. It wants to keep us safely in the old stories, in a world made up of anxiety and restless consumption. But that kind of world – the one that wants to quickly fix you and instantaneously connect you – cannot meet your wounds and your grief. The fact that you are hurting so much, that you are so restless and so dissatisfied, reveals the inadequacy of this world that claims it can give you everything you need.

To be clear, 'the world' is not everything 'out there' that is cruel and heartless and indifferent. It is simply *a way of being in the world*, an old story playing itself out over and over again. It's as much *in* us as *around* us. We internalize it without realizing; we believe in it. As the poet says, it is 'too much with us'. And, as he goes on to say, 'we are out of tune / It moves us not'. One of its products is the limited self that we take ourselves to be. When the old stories have failed to give us life and when our wounds and grief have been unacknowledged for too long, something happens. It happened to Hamlet and he ended up 'weary, stale and flat'. When it happens to us, we might well say that we're depressed. Finding ourselves in *this* desert will feel like the worst thing that could have happened. But it might be the best. There are those who have gone before us into this forbidding territory. They went into a real, sand-covered, rocky wilderness – and discovered that it is a place of transformation. They show us that we can indeed *find ourselves* in the desert.

FATHERS AND MOTHERS

In the Middle East of the third and fourth centuries ever-increasing numbers of men and women chose to leave the cities of Egypt, Palestine and Syria and move to the desert. These are the early Christians who became known as the Desert Fathers and Mothers. They were the first monks and some of the earliest meditators. They put themselves into voluntary exile in the inhospitable deserts because they were convinced that they could not lead authentic lives amid the distractions and dishonesty of the cities that made up 'the world'. They wanted to live in the kingdom, embodying the teachings of Jesus. But they were wise enough to know that this wasn't accomplished by simply turning your back on one 'evil' world and embracing another much 'holier' one. They knew they were making a radical commitment to seeking out self-knowledge and following it wherever it led them. They knew (or they soon found out) that this wasn't going to be easy and was almost certainly going to be a painful struggle. The goal was not to become saintly or models of Christian perfection. It was something much more realistic and urgent than that. It was also practical and personal. Poemen, one of the most celebrated of the Desert Fathers, sums up what they were about, in his advice to a fellow inhabitant of the wilderness: 'Teach your mouth to say that which you have in your heart.'

The abba's recommendation may at first glance look like a modest, even a rather quaint, piece of encouragement. Followed through, though, it is difficult to see what could be of higher value for a human being to learn. It begins to look like the very essence of sanity, and the doorway to peace. There is no need to seek further. This daily commitment to the harmonizing of inner and outer life *is* the salvation, redemption and forgiveness that others might just theorize or perhaps pray about. These people were determined to live it.

As soon as I discovered the Desert Fathers and Mothers (in a book by Thomas Merton, where else?) they exerted a powerful attraction. I was struck by their relentless dedication to an honest exploration of who they were, and who they were *not*. They seemed determined to bring everything out into the open, into the bright light of the desert, putting an end to illusion and self-deception. It was all to be done, not through abstract reasoning or scholastic philosophy, but through the messy business of living alone-together in shared solitude with the neighbour. Above all was the constant reminder and supreme value of the desert communities: to suspend any judgements that you are tempted to make on yourself and on others:

Go, do not neglect your prayer, and speak ill of no one.

Wherever you go, do not judge yourself and you will be at peace.

Their teaching was their lives and their lives were their teaching. They already knew that *Life is the treatment!*

It wasn't just me who found the Desert Fathers and Mothers irresistible. Something about their whole-hearted approach makes a clear appeal to contemporary sensibilities. It's to do with their emphasis on the personal, the local, the experiential and the ordinary. These were not extraordinary people in the sense that they were sophisticated or highly educated. Many were peasants, traders, shepherds – even former slaves and prostitutes. They were, though, ordinary people doing extraordinary things, and reminding us what we are all capable of.

Also appealing is the desert-dwellers' preference to teach – even that may be too cumbersome a word for them – to *show* using concrete stories rather than abstract principles. And to address the specific situation of each particular person seeking guidance at that particular time. No generalities, no idealization, no high-and-mighty aspirations; just a relentless, and relentlessly forgiving, attention to *what is*. This constantly renewed commitment to what Merton describes as 'a clear, unobstructed vision of the true state of affairs' would have made the desert-dwellers counter-cultural wherever and whenever they existed. In many ways they anticipate the dissenting social movements and experiments in communal living that arose in the West in the 1960s. There are also particular aspects of their undertaking that have led many to describe the

Desert Fathers and Mothers as the very first practising psychologists. I'd go further and add that they also speak to us as representatives of the earliest ever self-help movement. For, although much of their time was spent in prayerful solitude, it is also clear that this all took place within the context of an implied and extended community. At the heart of their experiment lay this truth: that the way to salvation was to be found in the encounter with our brothers and sisters (*how we treat each other*). Or, as Abba Anthony, the most celebrated of these early monks says, even more directly: 'Our life and our death is with our neighbour.'

Before there can be this 'clear unobstructed vision of the true state of affairs', there needs to be self-knowledge. Self-knowledge can only be gained by a recognition of what is obstructing our vision and what is keeping us in chains. For the Desert Fathers and Mothers this was nothing other than the urgent matter of what was keeping them out of the kingdom and what was denying them their sanity. Wisely, they understood that these two were the same thing. Above all, what they sought was *quies* – rest. Not holy floating, but the gift of being at realistic peace even in the middle of suffering and distress. As ever, the process of taming and befriending 'the enemy' that was getting in the way involved a process of naming (identifying) and un-naming (letting it go, giving up). The names in question were provided by a Desert Father who has his own unforgettable handle: Evagrius Ponticus.

Among the monks, most of whom were illiterate, Evagrius stood out as a highly educated classical scholar. Once he had shared long enough in the stripped-down life of the desert he was moved to offer a systematized account of just what it was that he saw getting in the way of the seeker after 'purity of heart' (which we can best understand as *clarity of consciousness* or – even easier – *sanity*). Evagrius identified eight deadly thoughts, which he described as the *logismoi*. Some translators offer t*houghts* as the best rendering of what Evagrius was after, but many others have weighed in with usefully nuanced variations, including *reason, calculation, reflection, fantasy, imagining, and obsessive preoccupation*. These all clarify and add detail to what is clearly the central experience that Evagrius is describing: that of being dominated and controlled by the relentless traffic of the mind. It's a kind of possession that steals us from ourselves. Evagrius named the eight deadly preoccupations as: Gluttony; Fornication; Avarice; Anger; Sorrow; Pride; Vainglory; Acedia.

Some of these need little elaboration. Others do, starting with the last of the deadly thoughts, *acedia* (pronounced variously as *aseedier* or *achaydia*). I've left this in its original Greek form as it is one of those potent words so beautifully nuanced that it all but defies translation. However, scholars and translators agree that the meanings it carries include *discouragement, carelessness, despondency, dejection, despair, listlessness, anxiety, weariness of heart* and *boredom*. (It is sometimes translated as *sloth*, anticipating its later positioning as one of the seven, when the eight deadly thoughts were edited down into 'sins'.) With *acedia*, it looks like we've stumbled across another of the many names of *depression*.

Looking back at the list of *logismoi*, we can hold them at arm's length as quaintly archaic and unsophisticated misreadings of the human condition; this is how we habitually patronize or sentimentalize the past. Or we can allow ourselves to be touched now by the direct wisdom of their teaching. Concentrated down to their essence, the *logismoi* present a catalogue of our attempts to fill ourselves up when we secretly believe that something (or, more probably, *everything*) is missing. *Gluttony, fornication* and *avarice* take us straight to over-indulgence, the relentless commodification of sex, and the forces of possessiveness, unrestrained acquisition and rampant materialism that seethe through our culture to efficiently invade our hearts, our minds and our bodies. *Anger* and *sorrow* are not deadly in themselves, but they can be when we allow them to fill us up, to become who we are. Which is what can easily happen when another form of attention isn't present as a check to the imperial ambitions of these unavoidable human passions. *Pride* is pride and always will be recognizably so: exactly the wrong kind of self-love. *Vainglory* is the relentless boasting and trumpet-blowing that often comes as the inevitably perverse expression of pride. Both are the signature of a self that has become full of itself, facing down the rest of the universe (where everything is an alien *other*) in an ongoing and doomed rearguard action to preserve this 'thing' called the self.

Each of these *thoughts* is one of the faces of a single deep impulse within the human psyche. The movement towards *filling up* the self is just a secondary phenomenon. What lies even further behind that is the fundamental desire to make the self (yourself, myself) safe. What is the doomed strategy that each of us embarks on to pull off this impossible trick? We try to turn the self (yourself, myself) into an object, a *thing*. Objects and things can be possessed. This is the root of our possessiveness, going way beyond greed and materialism. We want to possess *ourselves* – that is the prize possession. The problem is that if we succeed we will be self-possessed, but not in a good way, and our suffering will only increase.

The last of the preoccupations – *acedia* – is always waiting, ready to step in when the project of all the others has foundered, as it inevitably will. The programme of every deadly thought was to cover up any experience of emptiness, any inkling that the self is not enough, any sense of poverty of any kind. The idea was to turn the world and the self into something that can be grasped, made safe and held on to. Which makes it clear that the *logismoi* can also usefully be understood as the *possessions*. We attempt to turn the flow of life into one kind of possession or another, only to find that, as a result, we in our turn are possessed.

There is something different, though, in this final deadly preoccupation of *acedia* or *depression*. Unlike all the others, in this one the project of self-aggrandizement or self-repair now seems to have been abandoned. All that's left is sloth, listlessness, dejection and despondency. The fourth-century monks were only too familiar with it. John Cassian, one of Evagrius' students, describes it in vivid terms:

> Then the fifth or sixth hour brings him such bodily weariness and longing for food that he seems to himself worn out and wearied as if with a long journey, or some very heavy work, or as if he had put off taking food during a fast of two or three days. Then besides this he looks about anxiously this way and that, and sighs that none of the brethren come to see him, and often goes in and out of his cell, and frequently gazes up at the sun, as if it was too slow in setting, and so a kind

of unreasonable confusion of mind takes possession of him like some foul darkness, and makes him idle and useless for every spiritual work, so that he imagines that no cure for so terrible an attack can be found in anything except visiting some one of the brethren, or in the solace of sleep alone.

Evagrius himself describes how an attack of *acedia* 'instills in the heart of the monk a hatred for the place' (his cell, the desert, the monastery, the world), as well as 'a hatred for his very life itself'. It seems like an end to all striving and all effort; even distraction no longer distracts. It feels like the monk in the desert (you and me) has simply given up. This state of affairs can itself become another kind of dead-end possession; there's an overwhelming temptation to identify ourselves with our depression. Which is exactly why the wisdom of Evagrius, the proto-psychologist, leads him to list it as yet another of the deadly preoccupations. But he, and many others of the desert-dwellers, also saw that it could be a place of transformation and *metanoia* – turning around.

How did these dedicated seekers of self-knowledge encourage each other to give up without giving up? And how can they help us, now?

A CELL, A WORD

Younger monks or visitors to these wild places would seek out the senior figures in the desert, looking for guidance. Feeling lost or perhaps paralysed by the anguish and torpor of *acedia*, they would typically ask their counsellors, 'Give me a word, Abba' or 'Say to me a word, Amma.' The 'word' that the abba or amma gave would always be pithy and to the point. Most characteristically of these Desert Fathers and Mothers, it would always invite the questioner to take some practical action him- or herself. The action recommended might seem startlingly simple, almost childish. And yet, contained in all of the offered 'words', hidden in plain sight, was the encouragement to make a full commitment to a *practice*. There is something you can *do*; and it *will* be effective, if you do it with your whole being, and continue to do it with no holding back.

The most famous of the 'words' offered to a fellow-seeker came from Abba Moses, who said to one of the urgently questing brothers: 'Go, sit in your cell, and your cell will teach you everything.' When you hear a response like this, you can't help imagining that it wasn't the kind of answer the questioner was expecting. True wisdom is always challenging and wrong-footing, as in the story of the great man of arms who went to a holy follower of Buddha to be taught the Awakened One's great message:

> The answer was: 'Do not what is evil. Do what is good. Keep your mind pure. This is the teaching of the Buddha.' 'Is this all?' said the man of arms; 'Every child of five knows this.' 'It may be so, but few men of eighty can practise it', he was told.

The *practice* is everything. Fine words and good intentions achieve nothing. Nobody else can do it for you, and there are no shortcuts. But there *is* fellowship, encouragement, a complete absence of judgement, and a way that you can follow.

Very often, the question from the seeker is some variation of 'How should I guard my heart?' Having surrendered the cosy defences of regular city life, the desert-dwellers are now mercilessly exposed to the apparent fixations of their own consciousness. How not to succumb to the dreaded *logismoi* that tell me how everything I have and am is worthless, and that everything I desperately crave is out of reach? In today's language we would be asking how we are not to be utterly overwhelmed by the deadly thoughts that make up our depressions, our addictions and anxiety. How am I to keep my sanity? At the heart of the Fathers' and Mothers' responses to this, and to all other requests for guidance, is the one essential teaching of the desert. It fully embraces *Life is the Treatment!* and then takes us even further into the very core of that great insight. What the Desert Fathers and Mothers encourage each other – and us – to do is simply this: 'pray without ceasing'.

What can that possibly mean? And, whatever it is, how are we to do it when the 'noonday demon' of *acedia* has us in its grip: paralysed, dried up, seemingly unable to act? It's obvious that the recommended ceaseless prayer has nothing to do with pious sessions of stereotyped beseeching, hands pressed together, forehead creased with the effort of trying to change the world, or God's mind. It would be practically impossible to pray like this every moment of the day. If we're in the desert, in the fourth century or the twenty-first, we need to have a completely different understanding, and experience, of what prayer is. Fortunately, one of the Desert Fathers spelt it out, in the clearest possible terms, for his brethren and for us.

John Cassian was a monk who spent time with Evagrius and with other of the abbas and ammas in the wilds of Egypt and Syria. Like Evagrius, he was unusual in being a scholar and a theologian. But he was also intently focused on the daily practice which would bring about clarity of awareness: a recovery programme for the troubled and floundering mind. Having spent many years in the desert, Cassian headed into Gaul (present-day France) to found monasteries there. He also wrote extensively, and in his *Tenth Conference* offered his game-changing description of prayer. In it, psychology and theology combine to produce the most direct, personal and essential practice of self-help for those wandering fearfully in every kind of desert.

In his extraordinary chapter *On the Method of Continual Prayer*, Cassian makes it unambiguously clear that the practice he is recommending consists of taking a single word ('Give me a word, Abba') or a phrase, and through intimate repetition and attentive listening to allow that word to penetrate your whole being; to become your flesh. What he urges is something far beyond a mechanical repetition or a dutiful reiterating of the word just from the neck upwards. He wants us to allow the word – the mantra – to search out every part of our being, to change us at a cellular level ('Go to your cell …') and sustain us at every moment:

> Whatever work you are doing, or office you are holding, or journey you are going, do not cease to chant this. When you are going to bed, or eating, and in the last necessities of nature, think on this. This thought in your heart may be to you a saving formula …

To be clear, our fourth-century psychologist, teacher and companion is telling us that this prayer should not cease – will not cease – even when we're in the bathroom, attending to what we need to attend to. Just after this passage he goes on to insist that the prayer will not even stop while we are asleep. It will be with us and within us wherever we go. We can make it our home:

> This you should write on the threshold and door of your mouth, this you should place on the walls of your house and in the recesses of your heart so that when you fall on your knees in prayer this may be your chant as you kneel, and when you rise up from it to go forth to all the necessary business of life it may be your constant prayer as you stand.

The reliance on the mantra, or the formula, as he sometimes calls it, depends on it being something other than a thought. We thought our way into this suffering, but we won't be able to think our way out. And meditation *is not what you think*. If the mantra can be described as a thought at all, then it's a *thought in your heart* – which is a different matter altogether. What we are doing in following this practice is giving up all the possessions that we store so tightly in our heads and bodies and hearts, allowing a space to open up that we can trust: the kingdom, *sunyata*, emptiness. We empty ourselves in order to allow the fullness of life back in – and out. We begin to trust our heart again – not the place of sentiment or even passing feelings, but the core of our being and of every other being. Counter-intuitively we meet, and are met by, this place only when we cease clinging to everything that we thought we could make a real self out of. Once we start consciously to practise this, the ceaseless prayer – which was there all the time – flows on unobstructed. John Cassian explains exactly how it works:

This, this is the formula which the mind should unceasingly cling to until, strengthened by the constant use of it and by continual meditation, it casts off and rejects the rich and full material of all manner of thoughts and restricts itself to the poverty of this one verse.

Poverty is the key word here. Probably the most misunderstood word in the Gospel teachings. If we think of it as akin to the attitude of non-grasping and non-attachment that the Buddha taught, then we'll be getting nearer to its true meaning. The realization of our poverty is our way of getting closer to how things really are, to being more sane. If reality is not a cluster of objects and possessions but a dancing network of relationships, then what's the point of constantly grasping at it? Better to simply open to it and to know that, through the acknowledgement of this poverty (we don't – we can't – possess anything), the infinite riches of sanity are at hand:

How blest are those who know that they are poor; the kingdom of Heaven is theirs.

Having realized this over and over again, we can return to the 'rich and full material of life', including all manner of thoughts, knowing it for what it is, and better equipped to bear it – even to enjoy it. Another name for this experience is *humility*, the essential value proposed and embodied by these inhabitants of the desert. This is not the false project of lavish self-abasement and of grovelling to those 'better' and 'more powerful' than you are. That would be just another of the seemingly endless games of the ego – the defended and timid self. This humility is none other than the unseating of that limited and limiting self; a recognition that the view from the ramparts of the ego is very partial indeed. True humility knows that the ego is seeing a tiny, refracted part of the picture. It's only the heart that can begin to see (and be seen by) the whole, both in the desert and in the dark.

CHEWING SAND

The Desert Fathers and Mothers proposed a way of managing and eventually overcoming the demons, the *logismoi*, the thoughts, the symptoms, the conditions that plague us. Whatever we call them, we know what they are and what they do. They get in our way. The programme that the desert therapists offer has a classic simplicity and logic about it. To see its clear outline we need to befriend another couple of lovely ancient Greek words: *askesis* and *apatheia*. The first of these words is where we get *ascetic* from. But the original word – *askesis* – is a very helpful reminder that the practice it indicates need not have anything to do with extreme abstinence, frugality and self-denial to the point of self-harm. *Askesis* simply referred to the preparation that an athlete would undertake in readiness for a sporting competition. So the best way to understand the practice is as an *exercise* or a form of *training*.

Apatheia has nothing to do with apathy. (That's taken care of under the heading of *acedia*.) *Patheia* itself is the ancient Greek for *suffering, feeling, emotion, disorder* or *disease*. It gives us our *passions, passivity* and *pathology*. Putting *a-* in front of a word denotes *without*. So *apatheia* translates as *without suffering* or *without passions*. The desert teachers tell us that the *askesis* of the continual prayer of the heart will lead to the desired state of *apatheia*. But we must also stay real. No holy floating, no spiritual shortcuts, no anaesthesia, no denial, no head in the desert sand. It is unrealistic, and a misunderstanding of the inner life, to aspire towards a state of consciousness that is entirely untouched by the storms and the tremors of our passions and our sometimes chaotic thoughts. This would be a rather sinister dream of a meaningless *purity* – and the end of our humanity. Our pathology and our psychopathology will always be with us. But they don't need to be always in control. Through our *askesis* – our practical training and exercise – we can put them in their place: held and embraced by the infinite peace and generosity of the heart.

The project of the desert – although the abbas and ammas definitely didn't describe it like this – was an AAA programme:

- From *ACEDIA* through *ASKESIS* to *APATHEIA*

The much later medical model's version of this would be:

- From *DISEASE* through *TREATMENT* to *CURE*

I think the most helpful account we can come up with as (permanently) beginning meditators who have lived with, and through, depressions is this:

- From *ANGUISH* through *PRACTICE* to *SANITY*

It looks neat, and it isn't – of course. Waking up, and growing up, both involve the acknowledgement that there are no miracle cures and no magic bullets. If there were, there would be nothing for us to learn; there would be no healing. My favourite quote about the spirituality of the desert comes from a book called *Meditations on the Sand*. The writer describes the desert as 'the meeting ground' of God and humanity. The vivid image that he then summons up will feel devastatingly familiar to anyone who has trudged, seemingly endlessly, through the desert of their own bewilderment and incapacity:

> One then ventures on to these tracks because one is driven by the Spirit towards the Promised Land. But it is only promised to those who are able to chew sand for forty years without doubting their invitation to the feast in the end.

Forty years is the mythical and biblical emblem for a time that seems to go on forever. At the time – and it might just as easily be 40 days and 40 nights – everything seems meaningless, full of temptations and distractions: *logismoi*. It's the kind of time where time seems to stand still. The biggest temptation is to believe that all meaning has died and that you had best die with it. The most powerful of all illusions can thrive in this 40 years of sand-chewing: that death – and not life – is the treatment.

MEDITATION: WE DO NOT KNOW HOW TO PRAY

Prayer and love are learned in the hour when prayer becomes impossible and the heart has turned to stone.

Thomas Merton knew the desert well. The Desert Fathers and Mothers inspired his books and his way of life. He knew the desert of depression just as well as the chosen desert of the monastery and its daily practice of contemplative meditation. His words here go to the heart of the desert experience, and to the heart of what prayer itself is. Merton celebrates the fact that eventually we find ourselves with no resources of our own left to call on. It is then that we find the gateway to true prayer, precisely because we no longer have a clear sense of purpose or agency. We don't know what we're doing or how to do it. Being brought to this state of poverty ensures that we are no longer in control, neatly and efficiently organizing our 'spiritual' and 'transcendent' experiences. Because our own power has failed us it feels as though we are capable of nothing. That is the paradoxical blessing: *nothing* is exactly what we need to be capable of at the time of prayer. If I am confidently in charge of my own prayer, I'm still stuck in the possessive maze of my limited self, the ego. Abba Anthony expresses this with the true Zen flavour of the desert's clearest (and blessedly ungraspable) insights when he asserts that the monk who knows he is praying is not praying. It is the monk who does not know that he is praying who is *praying*.

This is seeing in the dark again. It can only be understood through practice. Even then we must stay humble enough not to understand it too well. As soon as we take possession of it, we have lost it. It makes as much sense to our everyday minds as does the experience that St John of the Cross celebrates in his *Noche Oscura*, The Dark Night. All his senses and powers have failed him and left him in complete darkness. He has no other guide or light than that which burns in his heart:

> sin otra luz ni guía
> sino la que en el corazón ardía.

It can't be worked out in your head. Everything has to fail us before true prayer becomes fully present. Merton even encourages us to open to the possibility that our distracted and despairing state might help us in prayer:

> And if your memory and imagination are persecuting you with a crowd of useless or even evil thoughts and images, you may be forced to pray far better, in the depths of your murdered heart, than when your mind

is swimming with clear concepts and brilliant purposes and easy acts of love.

The most important thing about prayer is that *you* are not doing it, *you* are not making it happen. There is a prayer ceaselessly taking place, which has nothing – and everything – to do with you. All you can do is withdraw your hungry attention from all the things you are constantly chewing over in your mind, and even below the radar of your mind – all the things you want to change, all the things that you can't leave alone, all the things you believe you can't live without. As you choose to place your attention elsewhere, letting it rest on the breath and the mantra, you are making less noise, fewer moves. You are allowing the prayer – which has never gone away – to be fully present in and around you, in the stillness and the silence. When we do this we are simply re-joining the prayer. We resume our rightful place within the prayer and recognize that in the end, and in the beginning, we *are* prayer.

What is this prayer? It is the endless outpouring of life itself, the effortless creative dance of Brahma, Vishnu and Shiva, the infinitely graceful flow of the Tao and the boundless play of inter-being in the emptiness where compassion and wisdom arise. The best way to say it is that *prayer is love*. When you pray you are not asking for anything or changing anything, you are simply stepping back into a never-ending flow of love and rediscovering that this is the only identity you have ever had or ever will have.

But 'love' has let us down before. Hidden in the anguish of depression and anxiety is the belief that love has failed. It may be that our experience of something we were told (or hoped) was love has left us with the deep wound of betrayal. Perhaps 'love' was surrounded with a set of conditions that made it impossible ever to trust it. Or perhaps love has simply been absent and the desperate efforts we make to *earn* it have proved sterile and confusing. This is the most arid desert of all. We are not acceptable; we are not *enough*. Somehow, the untruth we internalize is that we are fundamentally unlovable.

Your meditation is the process of becoming de-conditioned. All that is being changed in this prayer is the *pray-er*: the one who prays. As soon as you begin to stop naming everything in your experience and surrender all of your attention to the breath and the mantra, the silence and the stillness of the prayer emerges. In these moments the self is becoming the Self. It is a profound reset. You are being restored to what you always were. As St Augustine says, you 'receive what you are'. This is not something impossibly distant in space and time or inaccessibly buried deep inside you. This is intimate and instantaneous – closer, as the Qur'an insists – than your jugular vein. As the Upanishad says, this is the spirit that in silence is loving to all. The spirit that is in your heart. This prayer of love is completely devoid of conditions; it dwells within us and it is who we are.

Thank God we don't know how to pray. We would only diminish it. All we have to do in order to be lovingly *prayed* is to gradually abandon our defences against the radiance of this present moment. Trust is slowly re-learned. You have struggled for survival in a desert to which you have been exiled. Now, in meditation, you give up the struggle and sit, defenceless, in a desert of your own choosing. There is a world of difference. Now you are available for love.

Before meditation:

… the Spirit helps us when we are weak. We don't know what we should pray for. But the Spirit prays for us through groans too deep for words.

Romans 8.26

Meditate for 20 minutes

After meditation:

Let me not pray to be sheltered from dangers,
but to be fearless in facing them.
Let me not beg for the stilling of my pain,
but for the heart to conquer it.
Let me not crave in anxious fear to be saved,
but for the patience to win my freedom.

Rabindranath Tagore

BEFORE YOU DIE

The heap of whitened elephant bones in the room is death.

The desert of depression can seem endless. Merton himself was honest enough to talk about it as the place of madness and death. From horizon to horizon there is only the experience of mute isolation and unbearable pain. You want to end it. During the months that I felt annihilated by the partial loss of my hearing and the sound of snorting beasts that replaced it, I thought about death all the time. Looking back into the darkness of that period, I think it wasn't just a daily or even an hourly thought but a constant jagged backing-track to every moment of my existence. This new version of myself was unacceptable. Contact with others seemed dangerous and painful – I couldn't give a meaningful account of myself. My mind took over and decided that my life had already ended.

No book that touches on the experience and the meaning of what we have come to call depression and anxiety can overlook the death-wish that they nearly always bring in one form or another. While I was in the arena with the bulls of Bashan breathing down my ear, I didn't make active plans to end my life. I didn't go online to research it, I didn't put my will and my financial affairs in order. But I did have a strong sense that all of this was unmanageable – too painful – and it needed to stop. As a part of this, I fantasized many times about ending my life and about the different methods of doing it. The fantasies always blurred or faded to black before completion. Perhaps it was the equivalent of the way that we never actually die in our dreams. Perhaps the whole response was an important part of my coping strategy. Nietzsche (the same Nietzsche who talked about an 'illness full of a future') seems to have taken the same line: 'The thought of suicide is a great consolation: by means of it one gets through many a dark night.'

Suicide is one of the things that we find it most difficult to talk about. But we must learn to talk about it. Suicide thrives on the wrong kind of silence. We fear that by talking about taking your own life we are somehow putting ideas into people's heads. This is definitely not the case. If you are supporting someone who seems desperately unhappy and has no obvious interest in living, rest assured that your mention of suicide won't be the first time the thought has presented itself. In fact, mentioning it will be another instance of the power of *naming*. Thoughts and fantasies that remain nameless gather strength in the places where we hide them. If they are named there is the possibility of taking some power back from an impulse that had threatened to be overwhelming. When the terrible burden of this particular thought is shared it bridges the deepening sense of isolation. The Desert Fathers and Mothers relied on this process; they had no interest in what the later Church became preoccupied with – the confession of 'sins'. What they encouraged – like good psychotherapists, good counsellors, good friends – was the *manifestation of thoughts.* Much more practical, much more useful, and completely without judgement, the fear of which keeps us mute and alone.

The World Health Organization tells us that in the year 2000 approximately one million people ended their own lives. It also estimates that there were 20 million suicide *attempts.* Worldwide suicide rates have increased by 60 per cent in the past 50 years, particularly in developing countries. I offer these bald statistics here as a counterweight to the predominant experience that runs through suicidal thinking and planning: that of complete isolation and disconnection. If you are feeling suicidal it might feel irrelevant and scandalous to say it, but I'll risk it anyway: even when it comes to this ultimate act of saying NO – entertaining the decision to give up *and* give up – you are very far from alone.

The great majority of suicide attempts are unsuccessful. What is really telling is that most of those who survive describe the ambivalence they felt about their course of action. They believed at that time that they had simply run out of options. They are glad to have another chance. Some attempts are more obviously impulsive than others, often fuelled by drugs or alcohol. But looked at with the widest of possible gazes, nearly every suicide is in one sense impulsive. It is something that happens when we are not in our right minds. We have come to believe that we are not capable of playing a longer game. This is not to heap further blame on the person who takes his or her own life. I understand why unbearable pain is unbearable. And I respect the right of those with terrifying terminal medical conditions to take the measured decisions that some countries allow them to.

I am only thinking out loud with you in this way because suicide has touched me deeply, in my family and among my friends, and I want to do everything in my power to make sure that we can all be held and sustained until we see the possibility of other options.

Meditation can be a part of this holding and sustenance; equally it may be a practice of utter irrelevance (or impossibility) at a time when you, or someone you are concerned about, are distressed to the point of considering suicide. The 'word' that the Desert Father in me wants to offer now are simple words of encouragement. *Connect*, and above all *talk* to someone, **no matter how pointless it may seem to you at this time**. If you are supporting or caring for someone, encourage them to speak, to name what is going on. Counsellors, therapists, helplines, friends and friendly strangers – they are part of life, and life is the treatment, and life is much, much bigger than anything we can think.

There is every chance that you or the person you love and support will discover the obvious truth that it's not *you* that you wanted to put an end to – it was the suffering. If we can slow down and know – like the desert-dwellers – that we are neighbours and that our life and our death is with our neighbour, there is the possibility that we will be shown other options. Hidden within a person considering how to die is a person who is really considering how to live. A good friend of mine who is a suicide prevention trainer once summed up what we all need to do for ourselves or for others when things get to this point. We must try, he said, *to give the world a chance to do something unexpected*. I agree with him. And there may be many kinds of deaths you have to die before you die. I want you to give up without giving up.

COMMUNITY

I began to feel better so I started going back to my weekly meditation group more regularly. Or: I started going back to my weekly meditation group more regularly so I began to feel better. Who knows? It's impossible to unpick these things. Recovery is always an interweaving of many threads. There is no knowing which comes first and which leads to what. The only thing I'm clear about is that the key element is time. For us to be able to work *with* time, as opposed to the feeling that it's always working *against* us, we need patience – the ability to sit quietly, doing nothing while the grass grows by itself. This is what meditation teaches. We also need other people. It seems to be easier to practise being *no-thing* in the company of others.

However it played itself out, I came to make a strong link between the recovery from this depression and the always open, and always holding, space that the weekly meditation group offered. Countless threads had supported me back to the group. As well as *treating me badly* (the thoughts of the ego in a huff) Life had been *treating* me via the love and patience of others; badminton sessions that revealed sources of energy I didn't know I had; the uninvasive touch of a complementary therapist; pointless but determined walks in the frozen countryside; a kind and attentive hearing therapist provided by the NHS asking what ailed me; trying to write …

I put myself at the mercy of Life with all its different faces and it did its playful work with me. In the end the release from anguish comes when we learn to play again. There is something about the fearful gravity of depressions that creates a world in which everything is full of a deadly personal significance but utterly devoid of meaning. Healing brings with it a benign reversal: a world full of meaning, no longer obscured by the relentless significance that you have found yourself scrawling all over it. There's an old joke that various nations tell against each other. I'm from England, so I'll give you the English/Irish version, as the joke is on the English. Two army officers in the same trench at the front line of battle are asked to give a situation report. The English officer wires back: 'Situation serious but not desperate.' The Irish officer, reporting on the exact same state of affairs, sends his message: 'Situation desperate but not serious.' I like this joke because a superficial reading invites laughter at the *silly Irishman*. But the almost instantaneous second wave that all the best jokes have comes with the recognition that his is the greater wisdom. The Irish officer's reply is pure Zen. *Desperate but not serious* sums up the pivotal recognition of our healing. It's another face of giving up without giving up. We need people around us and a practice that can help us to do that.

Even though I was sometimes reluctant to go to it, the meditation group was a home for me: a refuge and a resource. I rediscovered that truth every time I went back. I could spend a whole day in fearful indecisive blankness, feeling empty of everything (including *emptiness*), only to find myself gently and mysteriously restored by the time the group drew to an end an hour and a half later. I was reminded who I was by the unconditional generosity of the other members of the group. Although I was sure that they tried to be kind people in their lives anyway, it was clear to me that this generosity grew out of our shared practice of meditation. In order to know who I was (and for them to know who they were) we gave up the self-defeating project of busy self-creation and self-maintenance for 25 minutes every Wednesday evening in an old Norfolk barn. We chose, in Hildegard of Bingen's wonderful description of prayer, to do nothing but inhale and exhale the spirit of the universe together.

We were there, following in the sandy footsteps of the Desert Fathers and Mothers, because of the teaching of an Anglo-Irish Benedictine monk. John Main (1926–82) was also in the course of his life a soldier, a diplomat, a professor and a Catholic priest. While posted to Malaya during the Emergency of the 1950s, he met an Indian monk, Swami Satyananda, with whom he learned to meditate. When he himself became a monk in 1958 he was instructed to stop his meditation practice as it was deemed to be 'un-Christian'. Years later, his study of the Desert Fathers led him to John Cassian's teaching on 'pure prayer' and the transformative practice of the recitation of the 'formula' or single verse. John Main called it the *mantra* and started to meditate again. He recognized that meditation was indeed Christian and that it was universal. There is no wisdom tradition that hasn't been led to this common language of stillness, simplicity and silence.

In 1975 John Main set up a Christian meditation centre, first in London and then in Montreal. After his death the

World Community for Christian Meditation formally came into being in 1991 under the spiritual leadership of Laurence Freeman – also a Benedictine monk – who had been taught for many years by Father John. Now – in 2018 – the community has become what it describes as 'a global and inclusive contemplative family'. It has a presence in over 120 countries around the world, supporting thousands of meditation groups – all in settings immensely different from our Norfolk barn, but each with the same core of trusting silence at its heart. John Main set out the vision, which continues to grow. He described this vibrant global network of practitioners as 'a monastery without walls'. It brings the living tradition of contemplation directly into the challenging desert of contemporary life. Everyone can do it – the practice is completely demystified and demystifying. There are no worthiness tests. Once you have meditated in this tradition, you are a member of the community. Any one of us can be a 'monk without walls'. And how to be a monk? The Desert Fathers and Mothers knew best. When asked the question Abba Poemen advises this: 'Say at every moment, "Who am I?" and judge no one.'

The community, following the teaching of St Benedict, commits to being a 'school of love'. Which inevitably means following the paths of contemplation *and* action together. One of the great learnings is that neither contemplation nor action is truly itself without the presence of the other. These 'others' are, in truth, one. So the community has given rise to an ongoing programme emphasizing inter-faith practice and a commitment to the growth of social justice. In 1994 the annual John Main Seminar welcomed His Holiness the Dalai Lama, who led an exploration of the light that the teaching of the Gospels and the insights of the Dharma shed on each other. This resulted in an ongoing series of dialogues between His Holiness and Father Laurence Freeman: *The Way of Peace*. The conversations have taken place in the UK, Italy, India and, perhaps most significantly, in Northern Ireland, where over three thousand participants of all faiths and none, including leading politicians, came together in 2000 to meditate and to work for peace. The Community supports meditation groups that meet in prisons, hospitals and homelessness projects. There are, as well, specific initiatives offering meditation as part of the recovery from addiction or mental health problems, including depression. There are also extensive programmes introducing and supporting meditation in schools around the world, as well as within the professional structures of business and medicine.

This is the community I didn't know I was joining, the first time I meditated with a group in 1999. Looking back across this gulf of years, I strongly suspect that there were two primary motivations driving me in search of a meditation practice. The first was a simple desire for survival. I was grieving – seriously *and* desperately – the recent death of a very dear friend, someone who seemed to me – although I didn't know the phrase at the time – to 'pray without ceasing'. I had never met anyone whose life appeared to be so naturally turned towards the Spirit. All through our friendship I bathed in the pool of prayer that I felt played around her wherever she went. (She wasn't, by the way, holy or pious – she was a lot of fun.) It was she who took me to L.A. to listen to Jim Finley and the silence. With her death I felt utterly bereft – I realized that I could no longer slipstream someone else's prayer-life. Now there was some heavy lifting to be done and no one else could do it for me.

The second motivation was a little less healthy, although almost inevitable and certainly understandable. It probably boiled down to the same primary motivation as the first: my wounded self's desire to survive as intact as possible. (It's a phase we all go through; some of us spend a long time there.) I'm pretty sure that I was still in the market for an identity. The identity of a meditator, a contemplative who integrated the Christian mystical tradition with the Zen wisdom of the East and the Beat Poets would do me fine. In other words, I was looking for a spiritual shortcut involving a premature abandoning of my 'self' and the assuming of a contemplative identity. Clearly I hadn't paid close enough attention to Merton's writings. One of the keynotes that sounds throughout his books like a tolling bell is the reminder that grasping after any fixed identity (even a 'true self', which looks so attractive to the limited one) is always a shortcut.

So what isn't a shortcut? Fortunately, the practice of meditation teaches us just that, keeping us honest and offering further lessons in humility: *seeing things as they are*. We may approach meditation (or anything else) with the desire to appear distinctive, special or even exotic in our own or others' eyes. It feels like another way of becoming an *individual*. The popular image of meditation is still that it is something to do in a leotard, while looking beautiful, gazing out over a sun-flooded sea or a gleaming mountainscape. Usually by yourself. Because it's a way of working on yourself, looking into yourself, improving yourself. The beauty of meditating alongside others within a wisdom tradition is that you learn how impoverished and short-lived that understanding of the practice is. The self is offered up, not to be replaced by a super-self – just one more possession – but to be met by *another*. We are not truly ourselves until we find ourselves fully open to relationship. The practice takes us there. This is what John Main means when he tells us that 'meditation creates community'. It gives us the chance to find out for ourselves, in our own experience, the truth of what Meister Eckhart says: that *relation* is the essence of everything that exists.

In the last century a British politician famously claimed that 'there is no such thing as society. There are individual men and women and there are families.' It's tempting to turn that on its head and suggest that there is no such thing as an individual. Of course we are all different and unique expressions of the formless. It's vital that each one of us continues to take on our very own forms, becoming the person we have it in us to be. In Jung's terms, we must *individuate*. But even that word offers us a rich clue. It has its roots in the Latin for *that which cannot be divided*. Yet our culture has come to understand the individual as someone separate, divided from the community. We have forgotten the insight that there is no such thing as a person, only a person-in-relationship. And we overlook the counter-intuitive fact that, even at the most basic physical level, each of us is made up of connecting parts – we *can* be divided up. In April of 2018 the BBC website ran a headline saying: 'More than half of your body is not human'. The story revealed scientists' findings that only 43 per cent of the cells in your body are human. The rest is made up of a microbiome – the collection of bacteria, viruses and fungi that we carry with us and that are vital to our health. A professor from the

Max Planck Institute put it neatly: 'your body isn't just you'. It turns out that each of us *is already community*. As within, so without.

Meditation teaches us that real growth is towards a deep recognition of commonality with each other and with all that is. There is no contradiction here with becoming who you personally and irreplaceably are. The expansion towards union – breathing the spirit of the universe in and out together – doesn't wipe out *you*, with all your idiosyncrasies, depressions and joys. It does the reverse, connecting you with all the other countless forms that emerge from the formless. A celebrated phrase of Teilhard de Chardin, the French philosopher, priest and scientist (who went through periods of serious depression himself), sums up the dynamic of meditation: 'True unity does not confound: it differentiates.'

The emphasis on community doesn't mean that in order to recover, or to be a sane and valid person, you have to suddenly become a gregarious socialite. Some people are just not 'joiners' and choose a more solitary path. But solitude (a completely different experience to *loneliness*) is not the opposite of community. As so often, when we start to bring a contemplative mind to an apparent opposition, we find complementarity. For Thomas Merton a true understanding of solitude was the key to everything: 'There is one solitude in which all persons are at once together and alone'. And he warns of the consequences if this foundational experience is ever lost to us: 'When society is made up of men and women who know no interior solitude it can no longer be held together by love.'

This is the insight that led the Desert Fathers and Mothers, with all of their apparently solitary ways, to live out the truth that 'our life and our death is with our neighbour'. It is also why the Buddha seems to emphasize the Sangha (the community of practitioners) as the most vital of the Three Jewels alongside the Buddha and the Dharma (the teaching). In the *Upaddha Sutta* he contradicts his follower Ananda, who offers the opinion that fellowship is half of the holy life: 'Don't say that, Ananda. Don't say that. Admirable friendship, admirable companionship, admirable camaraderie is actually the whole of the holy life.' The same depth of understanding led John Main to describe the community that meditation creates as 'a community of love'.

VOICES FROM THE SILENCE

When I was invited to write a book on meditation and depression, my immediate thought was to turn to the community in order to tap into the real experiences of real people around the world. Over the years I had been to enough retreats, led enough workshops and counselled enough clients to know that, fundamentally, nearly everyone is drawn to the practice of meditation out of what the world might rather woodenly describe as 'mental health concerns'. We know that we are not in our right minds (diagnosed or not) and we look for the place where we hope to find some clarity and a measure of peace. We might well be after a quick 'cure', a stilling of our anxious distress, only to find ourselves launched on the long pilgrimage to sanity. We might not feel that we are getting anywhere, but we will have a greater sense of being accompanied. And that turns out to be what sanity is.

I thought that I was probably safe in assuming that many of the thousands of practising meditators who make up the worldwide community would have also had experience of anxiety and different types of depression. A widely accepted figure says that one in four of the general population certainly will. So I put a short article in the international newsletter of the community, which is also published online. I asked if anyone wanted to share their experiences of meditation and depression, then sat back and waited. Within a few days I had emails coming into my inbox from different parts of the world, including Australia, America, Ireland, France and the UK. These were all people practising within the tradition as passed on from Jesus through the Desert Fathers and John Cassian, through the *Cloud of Unknowing* and the entire Christian contemplative tradition, on to John Main and Laurence Freeman and further on through all the members of the living community who continue to find that the practice itself is the great teacher. My correspondents also talked about other forms of meditation that had been part of their pilgrimage into a deeper understanding of the self and of their relationship with others. These included the silent ministry of the Quakers, meditation within the Theravadan and Mahayana traditions of Buddhism, the discipline of Zen and the practice of Christian Insight Meditation, marrying Vipassana and Christian contemplation.

I felt profoundly touched and honoured as deeply personal accounts of struggles with depression, and how meditation could help – or not – continued to flow onto my computer screen as the weeks went by. I wept more than once as complete strangers talked about such humbling and intimate periods of their lives. I couldn't help but feel that here – in this honest and trusting readiness to share what we are usually only too ready to feel ashamed about – was the mark of a true and loving community. What struck me most of all in the stories from people in such different walks of life (including one nun and one monk) was just how realistic they were about meditation. Nobody made grandiose claims for the practice as the way to solve all problems. For most there was a clear-sighted awareness that meditation 'is not the cure for depression', along with reports of times when it would have been pointless or even unhelpful to try and meditate. Some understood their experiences as an illness, a condition that definitely requires treatment through medication and other medical interventions. They provided living testimonies to the compatibility of medication and meditation. Many others talked about the paradoxical terrors of the darkness and the riches that can be found within it.

This collective and hard-won wisdom, so freely and readily offered, felt like a real treasure to me. It came from people who were not afraid of looking at distressing and inconvenient truths. As we all do, they discovered that meditation *is not what you think*; they were challenged by it, and some talk about times when they gave it up. And yet all returned and continued with the practice, expressing deep gratitude for what more than one correspondent described as 'a gift'. It seemed to me that the best way to honour this treasure would be to let these courageous voices speak for themselves through the distress. Every one of them expressed in their notes to me how happy they would be if any of their words helped anyone else who felt alone and engaged on a dark and dangerous journey.

I've selected some passages from a few of those who wrote to me.

From an Australian woman

I had begun exploring meditation as a technique for reducing my anxiety but what captured my attention and continues to energise my practice is the possibility of meditation as prayer ...

When I first began meditating I hoped that it was going to be 'the cure' for my depression – I was highly motivated and committed. I had been on antidepressant medication for about three years and was keen yet again to come off ...

(She describes the disastrous effects of stopping her medication)

Of course I went back onto the medication much to the relief of family and friends and began the slow restabilization of my body and mood. During this time I continued to meditate – the rhythm has become firmly established – and my meditation was becoming my prayer.

Prayer prior to meditation was often an experience of cathartic drama, unsettled by anxiety. I routinely found myself banging on God's door, asking, tearfully requesting, defiantly demanding help – help for me, help for my family, help, help, help!! High anxiety correlated with high-intensity prayer. The gift of meditation has, however, slowly changed my prayer life – which is now not about talking and asking, but rather about listening: listening to the mantra, at times floating on a sea of distraction but somehow, too, immersed in the silence of God's presence.

From a man in the USA (a pastor)

Something that came to mind while journaling this morning is how meditation has helped me to accept depression. Accepting the painful emotional feeling that depression is, accepting the biological reality of how I am wired, accepting whatever may trigger a particularly bad bout of depression. Acceptance can be very liberating, but it is also difficult because it is acknowledging a limitation. I had to pass up a ministry opportunity that offered more pay but was more demanding. I tried it for a while but had to resign from the position after an emotional breakdown. I went back to a more familiar position for less money. This is my understanding of what Henri Nouwen calls downward mobility. It sounds very liberating when read on paper, and in practice it certainly does bring a measure of spiritual freedom. After all, you accept what you can and cannot handle and in the process remove yourself from the treadmill of upward mobility. Yet it is difficult to see peers and colleagues move on to more prestigious roles, to see people not bound by your limits succeeding and doing well.

From a woman in the UK
Through those times of darkness I did learn a lot about myself, and the likely reasons for the depression. I also grew as a person, having, and wanting, to persevere on the difficult path towards healing ...

Just to put it all in context, I have been a Christian almost all my life (now in my sixties) and began meditation probably after the time I experienced the first depression. I have continued ever since, except during the time of intense mental health (depression) when I deemed it both impossible and unhelpful to meditate ...

It was a very dark place. I would not have had the resources and energy to deal with anything that might have arisen from the unconscious in meditation at that time. Being so unwell, it was in a way too risky to meditate at that point – I did not want to risk emotional overload. I probably was not able to be attentive anyway. I was suicidal at times. (It felt afterwards as if I had virtually lost fourteen months of my life.)

However, I realised looking back how much it had taught me about the nature of darkness, how formative it can be, and that there are indeed treasures hidden in the dark places. I would not want to go through that time again. Yet the experience of emptiness was real and very instructive (afterwards!). And of course it gave me more understanding of those themes in the spiritual journey ...

I would say that meditation and contemplative prayer since then have probably helped me, almost without my realizing it, to keep that 'black dog' at bay. I think it enables me to stand back from my emotions and therefore to be able to process them more effectively rather than be overwhelmed by them. It gives my inner life a place to breathe, and has no doubt helped me to believe in myself.

From a monk in Ireland

Depression has been my companion on and off over the years. Owing to a major breakdown two years ago Brother Depression has decided to become more permanent. I call my depression a Dark Grace. It is a searingly purifying and transforming experience.

The prayer that sums it up most for me is: 'Out of the depths I cry to you, O Lord! Lord, hear my cry!' The mornings are not great for me now, so from time to time I haven't got in my morning period of meditation. There are times when I simply am so drained that I cannot face the meditation period. At times like that I just sit in an armchair and pray the rosary. I do practise the Jesus Prayer as I go about my daily tasks. My strategy now is to judge what is the least stressful approach or method of prayer at particular times and go with that. Sometimes I just nod off to sleep. If I don't get in my evening session while I am reasonably energetic then I let it go. I try not to beat myself up about this ...

By saying the mantra I am not allowing the negative thoughts and emotional patterns to overwhelm me! Its great benefit is that I am opened up to the healing presence of God.

From a German woman living in the UK
I could not sleep, could not eat, I could not focus on any written text and had soon withdrawn from all my family and friends. I was not in touch with my feelings at all, and yet I was in tears every day ...

My life has been transformed through my regular practice of meditation. I feel more fully alive and integrated and in touch with reality. I have come to see depression just as another illness (as it is in my case), and the fact that I have to take my medication every morning and evening is just another one of those health hazards as is high blood pressure or diabetes. But I know with absolute confidence that the path which led me closer to God is intimately connected with this time of trial which I have come to regard as a time when my thoughts and feelings were purified, and allowed me to be stronger than I had been before those events. It took much time and effort, and the loving care of my closest friends, but it all is a complete package, the package of my development as a person.

From a man in the UK
When I started meditation, which I took to straight away, I sat in front of my lamp for the required twenty minutes

and since this time I've had no return of the depression. You may conclude that this is due to the use of the lamp but although I haven't proved this (I wouldn't like to encourage the return of the depression) I'm convinced that meditation has helped tremendously. I feel more relaxed, focused and seem to make much better use of my time. Concentrating on the present and not worrying about the future or harping on about the past is definitely the path to take.

From a woman in Australia
I had trauma in my background where there was a lot of fear and stress (alcoholism and mental illness). Today, I say that if it was not for my background, I would not have searched for answers all my life and come to this pathway, which I am very grateful for …

I came to a point in my life when I felt meditation was my last chance. I first went to a group at an Anglican Church and when they changed their times and I could no longer attend, I felt angry, as if something had been taken away from me. That's when I decided to start my own group, and I cannot believe (oh, me of little faith) how the silence has bonded us and we are still going after seven years …

My depression has not disappeared. I feel it is early days yet and the ocean waves will always be choppy but there are definite deeper times of stillness, silence and simplicity which I have encountered and which encourage me to keep on the journey. My life is expanding and I am very grateful.

From a woman in the USA
My experience is that meditation as a form of prayer, as well as any other form of prayer, does not really work during the actual moment of a crisis. I doubt at the actual moment

when Job was losing his children that he was spending his time in silence. When experiencing loss or pain, it is difficult to cope and our first response is sadness and even despair.

So maybe meditation for depression as a helpful form of prayer takes on the repetitive mantra as a plea 'asking' God to quiet the soul, 'acknowledging' God's presence though not really feeling it, and making every attempt at 'waiting' on God for as long as humanly possible with the realization in the back of your mind and inside your heart that He has been there before and will most certainly come again.

From a man in Ireland

A set-back is a set-back, but a depression left one unable to function and I somehow knew that reflection and acceptance of the harsh truth of any situation was the only cure for depression ...

I remember the first six months of attending the group that I heard little of what was being said in the introductory talks. All I was interested in was the silence. It was in the silence that I found recovery. It was in the silence that healing happened. It was in the silence that the panic and fear left me and I became restored to good psychological health. It might have taken up to six months until I was better. I remember the day that I realised that a week had passed and I had suffered no physical or psychic pain. I was over my illness. Where to now? ...

When I first experienced joy in my life I didn't know what it was. I thought there must be something wrong at the back of it. But there it was: a sense of joy. A sense of peaceful joyfulness that pervaded everything. I was sweeping the driveway one Saturday morning when I was overcome with an all-pervasive sense of perfect joy. I ought to have been frightened but I wasn't. It has a sweetness of sensation, and a slow pervasiveness as if I had injected some powerful drug to induce such a powerful sense of wellbeing. I took my sweeping brush and went down to the church car-park which I had noticed needed sweeping and worked away for an hour trying to make sense of what had happened ...

The depressive lines of thought that were part of my personal history as understood by myself somehow faded, and the energy that had been locked in them somehow became available to me so that new interests and fresh energy made my life much happier.

I do not believe that meditation is the cure for depression. I believe that it can help to solve the difficulties experienced by the depressive. The greatest thing about the practice is that it is a discipline that can be followed on my own without chemical or psychological input from outside. I can be the doctor of my own disease. I can avoid becoming a patient: dependent on the dispensation of others. I have a practice that allows me to look after myself.

***

This is a glimpse of a small community – the people who wrote to me – who don't know each other and aren't aware of being a community-within-a-community. But they are present now whenever I meditate – perhaps we are occasionally even meditating at the same time in our scattered locations; in the truest sense, of course, we *always* are. In turn, they are a part of the worldwide meditation community and, beyond that, of the entire human family. They are a glimpse of *us*. No longer demanding a cure, but growing ever more open to the mystery of healing. We all come to meditation looking – sometimes desperately – for the benefits that it can provide. We think we know what we need; sometimes we are right and sometimes we even get those benefits. But beyond that are the unlooked-for gifts – those things that we could never ever think of or anticipate. They come, underneath the radar of our thoughts and our desires, almost without us noticing. These are the fruits of sitting, as patiently as we can, with an increasing sense of being accompanied, in the silence and simplicity that some call Spirit. St Paul was confident enough to name these fruits: love, joy, peace, forbearance, kindness, goodness, faithfulness, gentleness and self-control.

As you sit to meditate, or as you struggle to get through the day, it might often feel that your life is completely devoid of these qualities. But if you continue returning to the practice of meditation, encouraged by the knowledge that you are not doing this alone, I know that you will be in the presence of all of these fruits. Their seeds are already within you – they *are* you. Meditation is simply the activity of allowing the truth that is inside and the truth that is outside to unite.

There are times when you will feel like giving up, and you might give up many times. I hope I've shared some clues with you about how to do that *without giving up*. In reality it's finally impossible to give up completely, because there is something that will never give up on *you*, never let you down. The first of the fruits of the spirit embraces and includes all the others. Because it is not a *thing*, it cannot die, it cannot give up.

ANOTHER BEGINNING

We all have to begin again each day. It's difficult to do when you know that the day is going to last 40 years and you are setting out once more on a stalled pilgrimage into the same old cul-de-sac. That is when we need friends to hold the way open, reporting back from their own zigzag journeys. We need a practice to keep us on the way, and a prayer that holds us when we feel that we're just walking on the spot.

I wish you well with all my heart as you carry on giving up without giving up. I wish you a thread, or many threads, that sustain you in the desert and in the darkness. Whether it is fishing or yoga or gardening or singing or walking the dog or drystone walling or discovering acupuncture or friendship or just chewing sand or just waiting or meditating – or all of them – never let go of the thread. And if you continue with your meditation practice, don't be alarmed or discouraged if nothing seems to be happening. Don't forget that it takes *as long as it takes to realize that it takes no time at all.*

Meditation can be the way that you transform the prison cell of depression into the monk's cell that *will teach you everything.* It offers a shift from *nothing happening* to *being no-thing.* There is a world of difference. The practice will help you to give up your search for *the cure*, to let go of what you think you know, to sit still and begin to heal.

Thomas Merton has felt like a friend throughout my adult life and all through the writing of this book. His heartfelt prayer helps us all in each of our beginnings:

My Lord God,
I have no idea where I am going.
I do not see the road ahead of me.
I cannot know for certain where it will end.
Nor do I really know myself,
and the fact that I think I am following your will
does not mean that I am actually doing so.
But I believe that the desire to please you
does in fact please you.
And I hope I have that desire in all that I am doing.
I hope that I will never do anything apart from that
    desire.
And I know that if I do this you will lead me by the
    right road,
though I may know nothing about it.
Therefore will I trust you always
though I may seem to be lost and in the shadow of death.
I will not fear, for you are ever with me,
and you will never leave me to face my perils alone.

MEDITATION: THE GENERAL DANCE

Let's meet one more time – one of many – in the present moment. This is the moment that is always the same but never repeated; timeless but always new. There are impressive-sounding words that have sought to describe the unhindered experience of this present moment and its sometimes hidden radiance: *the kingdom*; *satcitananda*; *heaven*; *moksha*; or just *now*. People even write books about it. But the present moment is always local and always personal. It has a flavour, a sound, a sensation, a smell and a colour, a temperature; it has its pleasures and its pains. Your present moment, as you prepare to meditate – or decide that you'll maybe do it later – is *the* present moment. There is no other; this is it.

Remember to meditate with the whole of your body, from the top of your head to the tips of your toes. Let the breath and the mantra flood your whole being as they are given to you and as you let them go. When your attention wanders, bring it gratefully and gently back to the mantra and the breath.

To lead us into this next beginning, I want to share with you the least depressing piece of writing I have ever read.

At the end of his *New Seeds of Contemplation* Merton offers some haiku-like glimpses of this present moment, when we catch the echoes of the playful dance of creation in all of its newness and emptiness:

> When we are alone on a starlit night; when by chance we see the migrating birds in autumn descending on a grove of junipers to rest and eat; when we see children in a moment when they are really children; when we know love in our own hearts; or when, like the Japanese poet Bashô we hear an old frog land in a quiet pond with a solitary splash …

Then his book finishes with these words:

> For the world and time are the dance of the Lord in emptiness. The silence of the spheres is the music of a wedding feast. The more we persist in misunderstanding the phenomena of life, the more we analyze them out into strange finalities and complex purposes of our own, the more we involve ourselves in sadness, absurdity and despair. But it does not matter much, because no despair of ours can alter the reality of things, or stain the joy of the cosmic dance that is always there. Indeed we are in the midst of it, and it is in the midst of us, for it beats in our very blood, whether we want it to or not.
>
> Yet the fact remains that we are invited to forget ourselves on purpose, cast our awful solemnity to the winds and join in the general dance.

The last sentence still strikes me as the best possible description of meditation.

Meditate for 20 minutes

Or twenty years

Or no time at all

Whichever comes first

POSTSCRIPT

I'm adding these few final words to report something that happened in the course of writing this book. It would seem ungrateful and a bit perverse not to pass on the gift that I was offered.

Nearly twenty years ago my mother gave me a sapling magnolia tree. Grown by her neighbour, a keen gardener, it stayed in its pot for a few years before being planted out in the back garden of a Norfolk cottage. Summer after summer produced no sign of blossom, just plenty of broad green leaves. Then suddenly, about five years ago, the delightful blooms appeared. I no longer live at that cottage, but I visit frequently. Last autumn I found myself fascinated by the extraordinary seed pods dropped by this now thriving tree. They were red, waxy, bulbous – some of them looked as though they were about to be prehensile. They had an ancient, almost unnatural air about them. The ones that I was holding somehow reminded me of the livid red knobbly clusters that I'd seen on the beaks and wattles of some slightly grotesque-looking ducks and turkeys.

I gathered up a handful of the pods and was taught (via YouTube) how to germinate their contents by a horticulturalist in Oklahoma. You rub all that waxy red flesh off along with the creamy, sweet-smelling pith underneath until you have the seeds themselves in your hand. Small, hard and black, like shotgun pellets or miniature flying saucers. You place all of your seeds in a bag of moist compost, seal the top and put it into the dark and cold of your refrigerator for three months. When the time's up, you sort through your compost to find – with difficulty – these tiny black objects, almost indistinguishable now from the surrounding growing medium.

I found myself doing this at the end of January, when I was firmly locked inside the cold, dark fridge of my own mute despair. Woodenly, I remembered the Oklahoman horticulturalist's instructions – seemingly given in another life, another world – and followed them to the letter in my sullen numbness. I filled about six pots with compost and seed and set them by the window as I thought about the possibility of starting the tinnitus-delayed book.

Through the winter (that I knew was never going to end) I watered the pots and blankly inspected them for signs of growth. Nothing for many weeks. Then one day, one of the pots was dotted with the faintest hint of green. I watered it and nurtured it. Yes, there was definitely something growing. But still nothing from any of the other little containers, each one a perfectly round and featureless tiny desert. When I came back from holiday, the one shoot was continuing to lurch out of the compost on an impossibly thin and white stem. *Etiolated* had never felt such an appropriate word. It was just hanging on, barely strong enough to support the two minute green leaves that had started to sprout. I determined to keep it alive.

Still no sign of life from any of the other pots. Quite the reverse: just dead, blank earth. Clearly nothing was going to happen, so I dumped their contents into other pots where I might plant something later in the spring (if it ever came). But I persisted with the nurturing and cherishing of the one slender growth until the day came when I could no longer deny that what I was looking after was a nettle. Now a vigorous and healthy-looking plantlet, but definitely a nettle. Something perverse, or lazy, or just weird in me made me decide to carry on caring for it. If I was growing a nettle, so be it – I would look after that nettle.

A couple of weeks further on and it suddenly seemed like a pointless and idiotic thing to do. Bitterly, and with resignation, I grasped (what else would you do?) this burgeoning nettle and yanked it out of its pot of earth. To reveal, just underneath where my 'weed' had been sitting … a tiny, curling, pale green, embryonic shoot that was already displaying the unmistakeable leaves of a magnolia. Now, at the height of this English summer, the plant stands at about four inches tall, with three pairs of perfectly formed (and full-size) vivid green leaves, which seem, to me, the most perfect leaves I have ever seen. At the tender spike of the growing tip, another delicate pair is taking shape. Not only that, I am now looking after another five plantlets that mysteriously appeared in other pots. I had used the rejected compost to plant a few squash seeds (because the spring did come after all), and what came up alongside them – out of nowhere – were these extra shoots, all of which are now busy turning into miniature magnolias in pots on a downstairs window-ledge.

How this happened, I don't know, but I think it might have something to do with giving up without giving up.

Love,

Jim

NOTES

p. ix John 14.1.

p. 5 Darian Leader, *The New Black: Mourning, Melancholia and Depression* (London: Penguin Books, 2009), 4.

p. 10 John Main, *Monastery Without Walls: The Spiritual Letters of John Main OSB*, ed. Laurence Freeman (Norwich: Canterbury Press, 2006), 29.

p. 11 *The Essential Rumi*, trans. Coleman Barks with John Moyne (New York: HarperCollins, 1996), 109.

p. 13 D. W. Winnicott, *The Maturational Processes and the Facilitating Environment* (Oxford: Routledge, 2018), 187.

p. 14 Thomas Merton in Bangkok, 10 December 1968. Available online: https://www.youtube.com/watch?v=ywE6bhApcSk (accessed 7 June 2018).

p. 16 John 12.23–4.

p. 18 John Main, *Moment of Christ* (Norwich: Canterbury Press, 2010), 13.

p. 19 William Styron, *Darkness Visible* (New York: Vintage Books, 1990), 7–8.

p. 19 Thomas Merton, *The Collected Poems* (New York: New Directions, 1980), 231.

p. 21 Main, *Monastery Without Walls*, 118.

p. 22 'At the still point of the turning world', T. S. Eliot, *Four Quartets* (London: Faber & Faber, 1959), 15.

p. 23 Luke 17.20–2.

p. 30 Eliot, *Four Quartets*, 15.

p. 38 Job 30.16–17.

p. 38 Job 3.25–6.

p. 39 Job 30.27–8.

p. 39 Psalm 22.12–15.

p. 40   Psalm 38.5–8.

p. 40   Shakespeare, *Hamlet*, 2.2.

p. 41   Shakespeare, *Hamlet*, 2.1.

p. 41   James Boswell, *The Life of Samuel Johnson* (London: John Murray, 1831), 264.

p. 41   Quoted in Clark Lawlor, *Imagining Depression* (OUPblog, 2012). Available online: https://blog.oup.com/2012/01/literature-imagining-depression (accessed 14 June 2018).

p. 42   *The Bhagavad Gita*, trans. Edgerton Franklin (Cambridge, MA: Harvard University Press, 1952), 9. Available online: https://archive.org/details/TheBhagavadGitaPartIEdgertonFranklin (accessed 14 June 2018).

p. 43   *Bhagavad Gita*, 13.

p. 44   Gwyneth Lewis, *Sunbathing in the Rain: A Cheerful Book About Depression* (London: Jessica Kingsley, 2007), 21.

p. 45   Lewis, *Sunbathing in the Rain*, 19.

p. 45   Lewis, *Sunbathing in the Rain*, 26.

p. 45   Lewis, *Sunbathing in the Rain*, 71.

p. 49   'Became as nothing', Philippians 2.7.

p. 51   Eliot, *Four Quartets*, 48.

p. 51   *The Upanishads*, trans. Juan Mascaró (London: Penguin Books, 1965), 114.

p. 53   Ursula K. Le Guin, *The Unreal and the Real: Selected Short Stories* (New York: Simon & Schuster, 2016), 633.

p. 53   Genesis 1.3.

p. 54   Genesis 2.19.

p. 56   Bruce Chatwin, *In Patagonia* (London: Pan Books, 1979), 129.

p. 58   Leader, *The New Black*, 13.

p. 58   World Health Organization statistics. Available online: http://www.who.int/mental_health/management/depression/en/ (accessed 14 June 2018).

p. 58   Victoria Bekiempis (2011), 'Why one in four women is on psych meds', *Guardian*, 21 November. Available online: https://www.theguardian.com/commentisfree/cifamerica/2011/nov/21/one-in-four-women-psych-meds (accessed 14 June 2018).

p. 58 Dennis Campbell (2017), 'NHS prescribed record number of antidepressants last year', *Guardian*, 29 June. Available online: https://www.theguardian.com/society/2017/jun/29/nhs-prescribed-record-number-of-antidepressants-last-year (accessed 14 June 2018).

p. 59 George Cheyne, *The English Malady: Or, a Treatise of Nervous Diseases of all Kinds; as Spleen, Vapours, Lowness of Spirits, Hypochondriacal, and Hysterical Distempers, Etc* (London: Strahan, 1734), preface.

p. 63 'In many respects the discovery of antidepressants...', David Healy, *The Antidepressant Era* (Cambridge, MA and London: Harvard University Press, 1999), 5.

p. 63 'Depression, in other words ...', Leader, *The New Black*, 14.

p. 63 'But there are other voices...', see, for instance, Steven Pinker: *Enlightenment Now: The Case for Reason, Science, Humanism and Progress* (London: Allen Lane, 2018).

p. 65 Sushrut Jadhav, 'The Cultural Construction of Western Depression', in *Anthropological Approaches to Psychological Medicine*, ed. V. Skultans and J. Cox (London: Jessica Kingsley, 2000), 41.

p. 67 Matthew, Chapters 6 and 19.

p. 68 Matthew 6.33.

p. 71 William Blake, 'Eternity', lines 1–4.

p. 78 Leader, *The New Black*, 21.

p. 78 Simone Weil, *Selected Essays: 1934–1943*, trans. R. Rees (Oxford: Oxford University Press, 1962), 10.

p. 80 Leader, *The New Black*, 25–6.

p. 84 'Mature depressive...', see, particularly, the work of Melanie Klein.

p. 86 *The Essential Rumi*, trans. Coleman Barks with John Moyne (New York: HarperCollins, 1996), 174.

p. 89 William Blake, *Milton*, lines 42–5.

p. 95 Thomas Merton, *Thoughts in Solitude* (New York: Continuum, 1997), 27.

p. 99 'Holy floating', Main, *Monastery Without Walls*, 42.

p. 100   Simone Weil, 'Daydreaming', in *For Lovers of God Everywhere: Poems of the Christian Mystics*, ed. Roger Housden (New York: Hay House, 2009), 24.

p. 100   Thomas Merton, *New Seeds of Contemplation* (London: Continuum, 1999), 19.

p. 101   Bhagavan Sri Ramana Maharshi, *Truth Revealed (Sad – Vidya)* (Tirruvannamalai: Sri Ramanasramam, 2006), 4.

p. 103   Matthew 16.24–5.

p. 104   *The Dhammapada* v.153, trans. Anandajoti Bhikkhu. Available online: www.ancient-buddhist-texts.net/Texts-and-Translations/Dhammapada/11--Age.htm (accessed 19 June 2018).

p. 105   *The Collected Works of Chögyam Trungpa, Volume Ten*, ed. Carolyn Rose Gimian (Boulder, CO: Shambala, 2017), 7.

p. 105   Thomas Merton, *The Inner Experience: Notes on Contemplation* (London: SPCK, 2003), 5.

p. 107   For more on the pre/trans fallacy see, for example, http://www.integralworld.net/fallacy.html.

p. 109   Merton, *New Seeds of Contemplation*, 33.

p. 123   R. D. Laing in *Did You Used to be R. D. Laing?* Available online: https://www.youtube.com/watch?v=wzieL7_aY94 (accessed 19 June 2018).

p. 124   R. D. Laing, *The Politics of Experience and The Bird of Paradise* (London: Penguin Books, 1967).

p. 125   https://www.theguardian.com/science/2018/feb/21/the-drugs-do-work-antidepressants-are-effective-study-shows (accessed 19 June 208).

p. 126   Joanna Moncrieff, 'Challenging the New Hype about Antidepressants'. Available online: https://joannamoncrieff.com/2018/02/24/challenging-the-new-hype-about-antidepressants (accessed 19 June 2018).

p. 129   Matthew 25.35–6.

p. 132   'Psychological Therapies, Annual Report on the Use of IAPT Services – England, 2016–17'. Available online: https://files.

digital.nhs.uk/publication/q/1/psyc-ther-ann-rep-2016–17.
pdf (accessed 19 June 2018).

p. 136   Mark 4.26–7.

p. 137   www.mind.org.uk/workplace/mental-health-at-work/
taking-care-of-yourself/five-ways-to-wellbeing (accessed 3
July 2018).

p. 138   Eliot, *Four Quartets*, 27.

p. 141   Rabindranath Tagore, *Stray Birds* (London: Macmillan,
1919), 22.

p. 146   William Wordsworth, 'The World is Too Much with Us', lines 1–2.

p. 147   See, for instance, Tim Wu, *The Attention Merchants*
(New York: Alfred A. Knopf, 2016).

p. 149   John Chryssavgis, *In the Heart of the Desert: The Spirituality
of the Desert Fathers and Mothers* (Bloomington: World
Wisdom, 2008), 24.

p. 150   Columba Stewart, 'The Desert Fathers on Radical Self-
Honesty' in *Vox Benedictina: A Journal of Translations from
Monastic Sources* 8/1 (1991): 7–54. Available online: http://
monasticmatrix.osu.edu/commentaria/desert-fathers-
radical-self-honesty (accessed 20 June 2018).

p. 150   Thomas Merton, *The Wisdom of the Desert* (London: Sheldon
Press, 1973), 8.

p. 151   'Our life and our death is with our neighbour...', see Rowan
Williams, *Silence and Honey Cakes* (Oxford: Lion Books,
2003), 22.

p. 154   John Cassian, *Institutes*, trans. Edgar C. S. Gibson (New York,
1894), Book 10, Chapter 2. Available online: http://www.
osb.org/lectio/cassian/inst/inst10.html#10.1 (accessed   20
June 2018).

p. 155   Evagrius Ponticus, *The Praktikos & Chapters on Prayer*, tr.
John Eudes Bamberger, OCSO (Kalamazoo: Cistercian,
1981), 18–19.

p. 156   Benedicta Ward, *The Desert Fathers: Sayings of the Early
Christian Monks* (London, Penguin Books, 2003), 10.

p. 156 *The Dhammapada*, trans. Juan Mascaro (London: Penguin Books, 1973), Introduction, 22.

p. 157 1 Thessalonians 5.17.

p. 157 'Noonday demon', Psalm 91.

p. 158 John Cassian, *Conferences*, trans. Edgar C. S. Gibson (New York, 1894), Conference 10, Chapter 10. Available online: http://www.osb.org/lectio/cassian/conf/book1/conf10.html#10.10 (accessed 20 June 2018).

p. 159 Cassian, *Conferences*, 10, 11.

p. 160 Matthew 5.3.

p. 163 Alessandro Pronzato, *Meditations on the Sand* (London: St Paul's Publications, 1982), 45.

p. 164 Merton, *New Seeds of Contemplation*, 148.

p. 165 'The monk who knows he is praying...', see Cassian, *Conferences*, 9, 31.

p. 165 St John of the Cross, *La Noche Oscura*, lines 14–15.

p. 165 Merton, *New Seeds of Contemplation*, 148.

p. 169 Rabindranath Tagore, 'The Grasp of Your Hand', in *The Heart of God: Prayers of Rabindranath Tagore*, ed. Herbert F. Vetter (North Clarendon: Tuttle Publishing, 1997), 39.

p. 172 Friedrich Nietzsche, *Beyond Good and Evil* (New York: Vintage, 1989), 91.

p. 173 World Health Organization Suicide Data. Available online: http://www.who.int/mental_health/prevention/suicide/suicideprevent/en/ (accessed 21 June 2018).

p. 178 Ward, *The Desert Fathers*, 85.

p. 181 Margaret Thatcher, interview in *Woman's Own* (1987).

p. 181 'More than half of your body is not human...', *BBC News*. Available online: https://www.bbc.co.uk/news/health-43674270 (accessed 21 June 2018).

p. 182 Pierre Teilhard de Chardin, *The Future of Man* (New York: HarperTorch Books, 1964), 54–5.

p. 182 Thomas Merton, *Love and Living* (New York: Bantam, 1980), 15.

p. 182 Merton, *Thoughts in Solitude*, 97.

p. 183 *Upaddha Sutta: Half of the Holy Life*, trans. Thanissaro Bhikkhu. Access to Insight (BCBS Edition, 2013). Available online: http://www.accesstoinsight.org/tipitaka/sn/sn45/sn45.002.than.html (accessed 21 June 2018).

p. 195 Merton, *Thoughts in Solitude*, 70.

p. 197 Merton, *New Seeds of Contemplation*, 192.

SELECT BIBLIOGRAPHY

The Bhagavad Gita. Trans. Edgerton Franklin. Cambridge, MA: Harvard University Press, 1952.

Cassian, John. *Institutes and Conferences*. Trans. Edgar C. S. Gibson. New York, 1894.

Chatwin, Bruce. *In Patagonia*. London: Pan Books, 1979.

Cheyne, George. *The English Malady: Or, a Treatise of Nervous Diseases of all Kinds; as Spleen, Vapours, Lowness of Spirits, Hypochondriacal, and Hysterical Distempers, Etc.* London: Strahan, 1734.

The Dhammapada. Trans. Juan Mascaró. London: Penguin Books, 1973.

Eliot, T. S. *Four Quartets*. London: Faber & Faber, 1959.

Healy, David. *The Antidepressant Era*. Cambridge, MA and London: Harvard University Press, 1999.

Housden, Roger, ed. *For Lovers of God Everywhere: Poems of the Christian Mystics*. New York: Hay House, 2009.

Jadhav, Sushrut. 'The Cultural Construction of Western Depression', in *Anthropological Approaches to Psychological Medicine*, ed. V. Skultans and J. Cox. London: Jessica Kingsley, 2000.

Leader, Darian. *The New Black: Mourning, Melancholia and Depression*. London: Penguin Books, 2009.

Le Guin, Ursula K. *The Unreal and the Real: Selected Short Stories*. New York: Simon & Schuster, 2016.

Lewis, Gwyneth. *Sunbathing in the Rain: A Cheerful Book About Depression*. London: Jessica Kingsley, 2007.

Main, John. *Monastery Without Walls: The Spiritual Letters of John Main OSB*, ed. Laurence Freeman. Norwich: Canterbury Press, 2006.

Main, John. *Moment of Christ*. Norwich: Canterbury Press, 2010.

Merton, Thomas. *The Wisdom of the Desert*. London: Sheldon
Press, 1973.

Merton, Thomas. *Thoughts in Solitude*. New York: Continuum, 1997.

Merton, Thomas. *New Seeds of Contemplation*.
London: Continuum, 1999.

Merton, Thomas. *The Inner Experience: Notes on Contemplation*.
London: SPCK, 2003.

Ponticus, Evagrius. *The Praktikos & Chapters on Prayer*. Trans.
John Eudes Bamberger, OCSO. Kalamazoo: Cistercian, 1981.

Pronzato, Alessandro. *Meditations on the Sand*. London: St Paul's
Publications, 1982.

Rumi. *The Essential Rumi*. Trans. Coleman Barks with John Moyne.
New York: HarperCollins, 1996.

Styron, William. *Darkness Visible*. New York: Vintage Books, 1990.

Tagore, Rabindranath. *Stray Birds*. London: Macmillan, 1919.

The Upanishads. Trans. Juan Mascaró. London: Penguin
Books, 1965.

Ward, Benedicta. *The Desert Fathers: Sayings of the Early Christian
Monks*. London, Penguin Books, 2003.

Weil, Simone. *Selected Essays: 1934–1943*. Trans. R. Rees.
Oxford: Oxford University Press, 1962.

RECOMMENDED READING

Freeman, Laurence. *Jesus the Teacher Within*. London: Continuum, 2000.

Gordon, James S. *Unstuck: Your Guide to the Seven-Stage Journey Out of Depression*. London: Hay House, 2011.

Lozoff, Bo. *It's a Meaningful Life – It Just Takes Practice*. New York: Viking Penguin, 2000.

Nouwen, Henri J. M. *The Inner Voice of Love: A Journey Through Anguish to Freedom*. London: Darton, Longman and Todd, 1997.

Rowe, Dorothy. *Depression: The Way Out of Your Prison*. Hove: Brunner-Routledge, 2003.

ORGANIZATIONS AND RESOURCES

The World Community for Christian Meditation
International Office
St Marks, Myddelton Square,
London EC1R 1XX
wccm.org
For meditation resources: www.mediomedia.com

Mind
15–19 Broadway, Stratford, London E15 4BQ
www.mind.org.uk

Mind is the leading mental health organization working throughout England. There is a national centre and there are affiliated local Minds in every part of the country. The website is full of valuable information and support resources.
  In Wales, see www.mind.org.uk/about-us/mind-cymru/
  In the Republic of Ireland, see www.mentalhealthireland.ie
  In Scotland, see www.samh.org.uk
Many countries around the world have a national mental health organization (the equivalent of Mind), most of which will be valuable sources of help for all kinds of mental health difficulties.

There is a lot of information relating to depression and anxiety available via the internet. One of the best resources is this video made by Matthew Johnstone in collaboration with the World Health Organization: 'I had a black dog, his name was depression'; www.youtube.com/watch?v=XiCrniLQGYc.

For access to counselling and psychotherapy in the UK, go to the websites of the UK Council for Psychotherapy, or the British Association for Counselling and Psychotherapy:

www.psychotherapy.org.uk
www.bacp.co.uk

ACKNOWLEDGEMENTS

First and foremost, my thanks to Laurence Freeman OSB who suggested this book and who made all the right connections, as always. Also to Robin Baird-Smith for being the most generous and supportive of publishers and to his colleague Jamie Birkett at Bloomsbury Continuum for his patient and always helpful editorial work. I'm indebted to Nick Fawcett for the scrupulous and gracious attention he gave to the copy-edit. I'm very grateful to all the members of the World Community for Christian Meditation who wrote to me from many countries about their experiences of meditation and depressions; particularly to Niall Charleton, Margrit Dahm, Anne-Marie Doecke, Nancy Edwards, Vikki McDonough, Mollie Robinson, Roger Tradewell and Matt Waldron, all of whom contributed to the *Voices from the Silence* section. My thanks, also, to Ed Giszter for reading the text and for his irreplaceable friendship over the years. Finally, and above all, to Jan Batty, without whom none of this, and not much of anything else.

PERMISSIONS

Coleman Barks's versions of Rumi's 'The Guest House' and 'Birdwings' are used by kind permission of the translator.

Lines from *The Bhagavad Gita*, translated and interpreted by Franklin Edgerton, Harvard Oriental Series, volume 38, Cambridge, Mass.: Harvard University Press, Copyright © 1944 by the President and Fellows of Harvard College. Copyright © renewed 1972 by Eleanor Hill Edgerton. By permission of Harvard University Press.

Lines from *The Dhammapada (The Path of Perfection)* translated with an introduction by Juan Mascaró (Penguin Classics, 1973). Copyright © Juan Mascaró, 1973, by permission of Penguin Books Limited.

Extracts from T. S. Eliot's *Four Quartets* by kind permission of Faber and Faber Ltd.

In the United States of America, excerpts from 'Burnt Norton', 'East Coker' and 'Little Gidding' from *Four Quartets* by T. S. Eliot. Copyright 1936 by Houghton Mifflin Harcourt Publishing Company; copyright © renewed 1964 by T. S. Eliot. Copyright 1940, 1942 by T. S. Eliot; copyright © renewed 1968, 1970 by Esme Valerie Eliot. Reprinted by permission of Houghton Mifflin Harcourt Publishing Company. All rights reserved.

Extracts from *Sunbathing in the Rain*, copyright © Gwyneth Lewis, HarperCollins Publishers, 2002. Reproduced by kind permission of Johnson & Alcock Ltd.

NOTE ON THE AUTHOR

Jim Green has worked for many years in the field of mental health with both local and national organisations, the Open University and the BBC. He describes his decades of meditation practice as 'always learning to be a beginner'.

NOTE ON THE TYPE

The text of this book is set in Minion, a digital typeface designed by Robert Slimbach in 1990 for Adobe Systems. The name comes from the traditional naming system for type sizes, in which minion is between nonpareil and brevier. It is inspired by late Renaissance-era type.